Letters of
Hadrat Ali Murtaza
(R.A.A.)

Translated by
Muhammad Ayub Khan

KITAB BHAVAN
New Delhi-2 [India]

KITAB BHAVAN
Publishers, Exporters & Importers
1784, Kalan Mahal, Darya Ganj
New Delhi - 110 002 [India]

Phones : *3274686, 3263383*
Telex : *31-63106 ALI IN*
Fax : *91-11-3263383*

ISBN 81-7151-

First Print in India 1994
2nd Edition : 2008

Laser Typesetting at:
Laser Track
1784, Kalan Mahal, Darya Ganj
New Delhi-110 002 (India)

Published by:
Nusrat Ali Nasri for Kitab Bhavan
1784, Kalan Mahal, Darya Ganj
New Delhi - 110 002 [India]

Printed in India at:
F.M. Offset Printers
Kalan Mahal, Darya Ganj
New Delhi - 110 002 [India]

LETTERS OF HADRAT ALI MURTAZA (R.A.A.)

CONTENTS

PUBLISHER'S NOTE

We have the privilege of presenting the series of letters of the revered personalities of Islam. Prior to this book, we have already published the following Books of Letters:-

1. Letters of Hadrat Abu Bakr Siddiq (R.A.A.)
2. Letters of Hadrat Umar Farooq (R.A.A.)
3. Letters of Hadrat Usman Ghani (R.A.A.)

Now we have the honour of presenting Letters of Hadrat Ali Murtaza (R.A.A.).

These letters belong to a period which was most precarious in the Islamic History. It was full of turmoil and trial. Symbol of Muslim Unity and Dignity of Pious Caliphate was virtually thrown to the winds. Discipline, Rule of Law and Ummah's unity was replaced by complete anarchy in the capital Al-Madinah. A handful of young rebels had already perpetrated a 'coup' and the elders were simply left as helpless spectators. It was not only the Third Pious Caliph who was assassinated, but the entire institution of caliphate was blown to the wind and completely destroyed. In those tumultuous days, Hadrat Ali, the Lion of Allah took the reign of caliphate in his hands and had secured the Oath of Allegiance from the General Muslim Public. But this was not the end of the problem, nay it was the beginning of a new chain of civil wars in the shape of Battle of Jamal, Battle of Siffin, Battle of Nahravan and so on. This civil war shook the foundations of the Caliphate and soon moulded it into Monarchy.

In those perilous and troublesome days Hadrat Ali (R.A.A.) wrote these letters to his governors, commanders and companions. The bitterness of those days can be easily seen in these letters.

From the biographies of Hadrat Ali (R.A.A.) we learn that he was a very coll minded, erudite, wise and patient person. His decisions as a judge in the days of early caliphs were most judicious and thought provoking. His advices in the Majlis Shoora (Parliament of the Caliphs) were always found very sound and sagacious. In his personal life, he was very forgiving, forbearing and benevolent. He did not take revenge from his worst enemy in the battlefield merely to quench the thirst of his anger.

He was brought up, trained and educated by the Holy Prophet (S.A.W.) himself. So it was rightly expected of him to be a model personality, and he proved to be so.

But all these qualities are not reflected in all these letters. In some of these letters, Hadrat Ali (R.A.A.) looks a quite different person. It is very difficult for a layman to conciliate between the two personalities- one seen in the History books and the other in these letters. The least can be said that authenticity of many letters may be questioned. However, we have done our best to present these letters with full references. Now it is up to the reader to judge himself about the authenticity of these letters. In the circumstances these letters were written and compiled, it was perhaps more than enough to put them the present form.

We are indebted to our revered friend, Mr. Muhammad Ayub Khan, Advocate, who kindly rendered these letters faithfully into English and fulfilled this delicate responsibility in a praiseworthy manner. May Allah reward him for this great service.

LETTERS OF HADRAT ALI MURTAZA (R.A.A.)

(In the Name of Allah, Most Compassionate, Most Merciful)

HADRAT SALMAN FARSI (R.A.A.)

Hadrat Abu Abdullah, Salman al-Khair al-Farsi, (R.A.A.) was a native of Iran. Originally he was a worshipper of fire, later on embraced Christianity and finally entered into the fold of Islam.

His advice led to the digging of Trenches in *Ghazwa-e-Khandaq* (Battle of Trenches) in 5 A.H. Besides, he also participated in all the subsequent battles fought by Holy Prophet (S.A.W.)

As regards his knowledge, Hadrat Ali (R.A.A.) commented: He possessed the knowledge of the beginning and the end of the period of Prophet (S.A.W.) and his person is an ocean of knowledge which never dries. He further remarked that Hadrat Salman Farsi (R.A.A.) ranks equal to Hakeem (Philosopher) Luqman in the field of knowledge and wisdom.

The Holy Prophet (S.A.W.) had honoured him with the title of "Salman-al-Khair" (Salman, the beneficent). He was appointed the Governor of Madain during the Caliphate of Umar Farooq (R.A.A.). He was also a narrator of traditions of Holy Prophet (S.A.W.). Sixty traditions have been narrated by him. Since he passed a long time in the company of Holy Prophet (S.A.W.) and observed the judgements and decisions made on different issues during that time, his verdicts were obtained in cases for the sake of authenticity. He passed away in 35 or 36 A.H.

(1)

TO SALMAN FARSI (R.A.A.)

(Written by Hadrat Ali (R.A.A.) before he assumed the office of Caliph)

In the Name of Allah, Most Compassionate, Most Merciful

Undoubtedly the world is like a serpent, which though feels soft, velvety in touch, is highly disastrous (in nature). Therefore, the worldly things which may appear pleasing, be avoided as these are ephemeral and unstable. And maintain yourself to have the knowledge of whatever is in this world but abstain from those which provide only worldly gains. Because lover of the world may become satisfied on gaining the worldly pleasures; but adversely this world pays him back in bitter displeasure. Endure all the consequences you may be exposed to but do not get enamoured with this world as it being attractive, becomes also most repulsive.

(Al-Irshad, p. 187; Usool Kafi p. 137)

(2)

TO THE PEOPLE OF EGYPT

After the martyrdom of Hadrat Usman (R.A.A.), Hadrat Ali (R.A.A.) was elected as Caliph of Muslims. He summoned Hadrat Qais-ibn-Sa'id-ibn Ubaidah Ansari (R.A.A.) and directed him to proceed to Egypt as the Governor of the province.

He tendered him advice on various subjects. Hadrat Qais along with his seven companions proceeded to Egypt. On arrival in Egypt he sat at the pulpit and read the august letter of Amir-ul-Momineen (leader of the faithful) Hadrat Ali (R.A.A.) which he had brought for the people of Egypt. The scribe of the letter was Abdullah-ibn-Raf'e.

The contents of the letter are as under:

In the Name of Allah, Most Compassionate, Most Merciful

From the Servant of Allah, Amir-ul-Momineen (leader of the faithful) Ali (R.A.A.) to those Muslims and the faithful, whom my message is delivered.

Allah's blessings be upon you. I praise and glorify Allah. There is none worthy of worship save Him and offer Salat (salutations) to His Messenger.

Hereafter, Allah, the Glorious and the Great, selected the religion of Islam for his Messengers and Angels by His best planning and execution and sent the same Islam through His Messengers to his servants and qualified them with that religion and exalted them by sending Hadrat Muhammad (S.A.W.) as the Messenger towards them. He, the Holy Prophet (S.A.W.) taught them the Book of Allah and the wisdom, *Faraidh* (Obligatory Acts) and the *Sunnah* (Practice of the Holy Prophet S.A.W.). He united them so that they may not disintegrate. He beautified and purified them and made them gentle and soft hearted so that they may not practice cruelty and oppression. When he (S.A.W.) completed his mission, Allah the Almighty recalled him from this world. May Allah shower His Blessings and Mercy upon him.

Then after him (the Prophet S.A.W.), the Muslims elected two pious leaders (one after another) as his successors, who followed the Book of Allah and the *Sunnah* of the Prophet (S.A.W.). They adopted good behaviour and did not deviate from the *Sunnah*. Allah recalled both of them. May Allah be pleased with both of them.

After them such a person became Caliph, who

introduced innovations, thereby exposed himself of peoples' criticism. Consequently they derided his acts, pointed out faults against him and replaced him.

Thereafter, people came to me and took their Oath of Allegiance to me. Consequently, I seek the guidance of Allah, the Glorious and Great, and pray for His help to keep me firm on piety. Behold! It is obligatory on us to follow the Book of Allah and *Sunnah* of the Messenger (S.A.W.) in your affairs and strive to impress upon you to fulfil the Rights of Allah and follow the *Sunnah* of the Prophet (S.A.W.). Moreover, your well-being in absentia is also our duty. Only Allah is worthy of seeking His assistance. He is enough for us and also a good Protector.

I have appointed Qai's (R.A.A.) as Governor and sent him to you. You should provide him strength, help him and cooperate with him in his right dealings. I have already directed him to deal courteously with noble persons and suppress the instigators among you, to treat all the persons politely whether high or low. He is one of them with whose conduct I am satisfied and I fully expect acts of polite behaviour and good wishes from him. I pray Allah for both, myself and yourself, for performing virtuous deeds, good recompenses and profound blessings.

May Allah keep you safe and bless you with kindness and prosperity.

(Tabari, vol. 5, p. 227; Sharh Ibn Abi-al-Hadeed, vol. 2, p. 24)

MU'AWIYA BIN ABU SUFYAN (R.A.A.)

He belonged to a respectable family of Quraish and laid down the foundation of Umayyad Caliphate. He made Damascus the capital of Caliphate.

Hadrat Abu Sufyan (R.A.A.), his father, was a staunch

opponent of Islam before the conquest of Makkah. After the conquest, he, with his brother, mother and his son Hadrat Mu'awiya (R.A.A.) was late in accepting Islam, yet he became a strong and sincere believer. Holy Prophet (S.A.W.) had great trust in him and assigned him the duty of copying the Divine Revelations. He also narrated traditions received through Hadrat Abu-Bakr, Hadrat Usman (R.A.A.), his sister Umm-ul Momineen, Hadrat Ummi-Habiba (R.A.A.), wife of Holy Prophet (S.A.W.).

Hadrat Mu'awiya was a brave soldier. He was included in the army sent by Hadrat Usman (R.A.A.) in 19 A.H. under the command of his brother Hadrat Yazid-bin-Abi-Sufyan (R.A.A.) for the invasion of Syria. After the conquest, Hadrat Yazid-bin-Abi-Sufyan was appointed Governor of Syria, and when he died Hadrat Umar (R.A.A.) appointed him in his place as Governor. After the martyrdom of Hadrat Usman (R.A.A.), who was a near relative of Hadrat Mu'awiya (R.A.A.), he was very enthusiastic and passionate in claiming retribution of blood and demanded from Hadrat Ali for handing over the assassinators of Hadrat Usman (R.A.A.). Thus confrontation between Bani Umayyad and Bani Hashim developed, which caused great harm to Islam. After the martyrdom of Hadrat Ali (R.A.A.), he entered Kufa in 41 A.H. and took Oath of Alleginace in his favour from people. He remained in occupation of the office of Caliphate for about 19 years from 41 A.H. to 60 A.H. He died in Damascus in 60 A.H.

(3)

TO HADRAT MU'AWIYA (R.A.A.)

After taking the Oath of Allegiance from the people for his Caliphate, Hadrat Ali (R.A.A.) delivered sermon and came back to his house. Soon after Hadrat Mughira-ibn Shu'ba

(R.A.A.) called on him and said, "Amir-ul-Momineen (leader of the faithful) I wish to tender a few pieces of advice to you." Hadrat Ali (R.A.A.) asked him to mention them. Hadrat Mughira (R.A.A.) said: If you desire the stability of your Caliphate, appoint Talha ibn Abdullah as the Governor of Kufa and Zubair ibn-al-Awwam of Basrah and let Mu'awiya ibn Abi-Sufyan to continue as Governor of Sham (Syria) till, with the passage of time, obedience to you becomes binding on him and he becomes loyal to you. Of course, when your Caliphate gains stability, you will then have the choice to dismiss them or to allow to continue any of them according to your desire.

Hadrat Ali (R.A.A.) said,"I shall soon consider the case of Talha and Zubair. As regards Mu'awiya I swear, my final decision is "May Allah not show me that day when I may seek his help in any matter. However, I am inviting him to accord allegiance to me. If he accepts, it is well and good, otherwise I shall wage war against him." These words annoyed Hadrat Mughira and abruptly he stood up and went away.

Hadrat Ali (R.A.A.) dictated this letter to his chief scribe Hadrat Abdullah ibn Rafe' for Hadrat Mu'awiya (R.A.A.).

In the Name of Allah, Most Compassionate, Most Merciful.

From Amir-ul-Momineen (leader of the faithful) Ali to Mu'awiya.

Hereafter: If Usman was the right claimant (of Caliphate) and relative (of the Messenger of Allah (S.A.W.), I, too am the right claimant (of Caliphate and his relative.) Behold! Allah has appointed me the Caliph with the consensus of both Mohajireen (emigrants) and Ansar (the inhabitants of Madinah) and it may also be brought to your senses that common men follow me in formulating opinion, actions, likes and dislikes. Consequently it is incumbent on you to report to me immediately as I have called all the Governors to get their

Allegiance and Obedience to my Caliphate and to ask them to share the responsibility which has fallen on my lean shoulders and in lieu of which I have bartered my faith and trustworthiness. There was no way out for me but to accept the responsibilities. Therefore, no sooner you see this letter than report (by the Will of Allah) post-haste to me aalong with your high ranking companions.

(Kifayat-ul-Matalib, p. 58)

HADRAT MUGHIRA BIN SHU'BA (R.A.A.)

First he was a fire-worshipper, then became Christian and finally accepted Islam in 5 A.H. He was a very intelligent man and a companion of sound judgement. Hadrat Umar (R.A.A.) posted him to Iran as a special envoy for Iran where he talked with Rustam very boldly and intelligently. Hadrat Usman (R.A.A.) first made him the Governor of Basrah, then of Kufa.

When Hadrat Ali (R.A.A.) did not accept his advice that Hadrat Mu'awiya (R.A.A.) should be let to continue as Governor of Syria, he became unhappy with Hadrat Ali (R.A.A.) and became aloof from the State affairs. He did not involve himself any more in the State affairs. He died in 50 A.H.

(Mustadrik Hakim, 3:450)

(4)

TO HADRAT MU'AWIYA (R.A.A.)

It is reported that when Hadrat Mu'awiya (R.A.A.) received the letter of Hadrat Ali (R.A.A.), he sent a letter in reply extolling his own attributes. Thereupon, Hadrat Ali (R.A.A.) sent the following letter (in verse).

In the Name of Allah, Most Compassionate, Most Merciful

1. Hadrat Muhammad Mustafa (S.A.W.) the true Prophet was my cousin as well as my father-in-law.

2. Hadrat Hamza (R.A.A.) the chief of the martyrs was my uncle, and this fact is known to one and all.

3,4. Hadrat Ja'far (R.A.A.) who remains flying with the angels, morning till evening, was my brother, born of the same mother, as was made known to all by the true informer (the Holy Prophet S.A.W.).

5. The solace of eyes (daughter of the Holy Prophet S.A.W.) was my close companion and wife.

6. My and her blood, flesh and skin are close together as being one and the same.

7. From them came into being my sons, the pleasure of my sour, who were the grandsons of Holy Prophet (S.A.W.).

8. Is there any one among you who possesses these qualifications and merits.

9. I embraced Islam before you, in childhood, before attaining adolescence.

10,11. From the day that my relationship (as son-in-law) was established with the Holy Prophet (S.A.W.) I command respect and obedience from you.

12,13. (Keep in mind) Alas: Misery and ruin is destined for him, who will come on the Last Day, as a known enemy of mine.

(Lata'if Akhbar-al-Awwal, p. 34)

(5)

TO HADRAT MU'AWIYA (R.A.A.)

Hadrat Ali (R.A.A.) wrote the following letter to Hadrat Mu'awiya (R.A.A.) in reply to his harsh letter:

In the name of Allah, Most Compassionate, Most Merciful

Hereafter: O Mu'awiya I am the assassinator of your maternal grand-father, maternal uncle and brother.[1] I still possess that sword with which I had assassinated them. Neither

---

1. Grand-father (maternal), Utba ibn-Rabia, a maternal uncle Walid ibn-Utba and his brother Hanzala-ibn-Abi-Sufyan, all three were killed by Hadrat Ali (R.A.A.) in the Battle of Badr. Hadrat Ali (R.A.A.) and Hadrat Mu'awiya (R.A.A.) i.e. Bani Hashim (descendants of Hashim) and Bani Umayyad (descendants of Ummayad) were indulged in opposition with each other for a very long time.

(a) Their fore-father Abd-i-Munaf was a prominent personality of Quraish. Every year on the occasion on Hajj, the Quraish collected subscription from pilgrims to meet their needs and each item of work was entrusted to different persons. As such the provision of food and water, an honourable duty was entrusted to Abd-i-Munaf. When he died this work was given to the son of Abd-i-Munaf, Hashim, the great-grand-father of Hadrat Ali (R.A.A.). This annoyed Umayyah, the grand-son of Abd-i-Munaf and great-grand-father of Hadrat Mu'awiya (R.A.A.) Since Umayya was himself a rich person, he offered to bear all expenditure by himself instead of collection of subscriptions or donations from the pilgrims, if the duty was entrusted to him. But the offer was not accepted by Quraish. He felt ashamed on this decision and migrated to Syria (*Tabari 181:2)*

(b) There was also discord between Harab, son of Umayyah and Abdul Muttalib, son of Hashim. The cause for this was an incidence. A wealthy Jew named Uzinah was living in the neighbourhood of Abdul Muttalib. He was a sincere friend and associate of Abdul Muttalib. He provided not only financial but every kind of help. Harab disliked this relation out of rivalry. Therefore he instigated a few youths of Quraish to kill the Jew and seize his wealth. The youth agreed to the proposal and after killing the Jew, took his wealth and went in the protection of Harab. Abdul Muttalib reproached Harab and demanded to hand over the wealth and the killers to him. This created bitterness between the parties, but Abdul Muttalib at last succeeded and Harab had to return the wealth

I have changed my sword with any other sword nor my Sustainer with any other Sustainer nor replaced my Prophet (S.A.W.) with any other prophet. Now do all that you could desire, (Allah willing) you will find me a valiant soldier. I am ready to fight any transgressor or misled.

(Lata'if Akhbar-al-Awwal, p. 350)

(6)

TO HADRAT MU'AWIYA (R.A.A.)

In the Name of Allah, Most Compassionate, Most Merciful

From the Servant of Állah, Ali Amir-ul-Momineen to Mu'awiya Ibn Abi-Sufyan.

Blessing (of Allah) be on the followers of Truth. I glorify Allah Who is the Only Worthy of worship and none else.

---

and also pay the blood money.

(c) During the Battle of Badr, the grand-father of Hadrat Mu'awiya (R.A.A.) Utba ibn-Rabia, who was a famous and brave warrior of Mecca along with his son Walid and four grandsons (maternal) Hanzala, Amr, Yazid and Mu'awiya (R.A.A.) arrayed before the Prophet (S.A.W.) for fight, out of them Utba, Walid and Hanzala were killed by Hadrat Ali (R.A.A.), Amr and Yazid were arrested and Hadrat Mu'awiya (R.A.A.) saved his life with great difficulty by escaping from there. *(Sirah Ibn Hasham 82:1)*

(d) The father of Hadrat Mu'awiya (R.A.A.) Abu Sufyan (R.A.A.) came as chief of Ahzab in front of the Prophet (S.A.W.) in the Battle of Ahzab (Battle of Khandaq 5 A.H.) *(Tabaqat ibn Sa'ad).*

(e) In the Battle of Uhud, Hindah, mother of Mu'awiya chewed the liver of Hadrat Hamza (R.A.A.).

(f) When at the time of assumption of office of Caliphate by Hadrat Abu Bakr (R.A.A.) Hadrat Abu Sufyan (R.A.A.), father of Mu'awiya (R.A.A.) tried to excite Bani Hashim. Hadrat Ali (R.A.A.) rebuked him that his advice was not required as he wanted to divide Muslims. *(Tabari, p. 202:3)*

(9) There had always been conflict between Hadrat Mu'awiya (R.A.A.) and Hadrat Ali (R.A.A.).

Well now! You have fully observed treatment of the world with its inhabitants, its effect, its import and its adverse behaviour with them. The best acquisition in the world is that which virtuous people get by observing piety and one who considers the Hereafter like this world, will find them poles apart.

Mu'awiya! ponder over it again. You have claimed a thing to which you neither deserved before nor now. You can neither present any well-established sound argument in its favour, nor produce any witness in its support. You are quoted neither in any verse of the Book of Allah nor in any covenant of the Holy Prophet (S.A.W.). What will you do when this worldly cloak which you have put on, will be deprived, whose beauty has captivated you and whose pleasure has charmed you. It has opened a path between you and your enemy (Satan). That enemy is highly misguiding, fatal and destructive. It has firmly fixed his steps in your soul. He extended you his invitation, and you have accepted it. Wherever he led you, you moved on and whatever order he gave, you obeyed. Beware! Leave him for good and care for your accountability, because soon you will find yourself standing at a place, where no shield could protect you.

O Mu'awiya! Recollect, have you ever been the leader of Muslim Ummah or the head of Islamic state? You have neither any previous achievement in your nation, nor possessed any past dignity. Therefore, rise from slumber and refer to your Creator. Be prepared for that adversity (Reckoning of the Last Day) which you will have to confront soon after. Do not let yourself be overpowered by Satan, whose evil nature has imbibed revolt in you. Moreover, I also inform you that Allah and his Messenger (S.A.W.) are true (who pointed out Satan as the enemy of man). We seek Allah's protection from that old wretchedness (with which you are involved).

If you do not comply (with my instructions) I shall teach

you a good lesson. You have become absolutely absurd. Satan has overpowered you. It is Satan which is running in your arteries in place of blood. You are neither the Imam of this Ummah nor its ruler.

As you know full well, had this Caliphate been under the control or authority of certain people, they would have envied us and boasted of their favour on us. But it was Allah's decision Who conferred on us (this office) and He got it reserved for us through the tongue of True and Veracious Prophet (S.A.W.). Now whoever knowingly and being fully aware of this fact doubts it, he cannot get success.

O Lord, Decide between us and our enemies.

Verily, Thou art the best of all Judges.

(Kitab Siffin, p. 48; Nahj-al-Balaghah, vol. 2, p. 7)

(7)

TO HADRAT MU'AWIYA (R.A.A.)

When the Syrians expressed their intention to extend their help and side with Hadrat Mu'awiya (R.A.A.), Hadrat Abu Muslim Khaulani (R.A.A.), a renowned divine of Syria, called on Hadrat Mu'awiya (R.A.A.) along with some other divines. He said, "It has come to my knowledge that you (Hadrat Mu'awiya R.A.A.) intend to fight with Hadrat Ali (R.A.A.)." He pointed out to him, "How can you (Hadrat Mu'awiya R.A.A.) fight with Hadrat Ali (R.A.A.) while you are no match to him." Hadrat Mu'awiya (R.A.A.) said that he made no claim of superiority in virtue and greatness over him. But he asked whether he knew that Hadrat Usman (R.A.A.) was martyred in a pitiable condition. Abu Muslim (R.A.A) replied, "I know." Hadrat Mu'awiya then said, "So it is proper for Hadrat Ali (R.A.A.) to hand over (Hadrat Usman's R.A.A.) assassinators to us, then I will surrender the Caliphate to him."

After this talk Hadrat Abu Muslim Khaulani (R.A.A.) said, "Alright! you write a letter to Hadrat Ali (R.A.A.) about this matter, and I will personally deliver this letter to him." Hadrat Mu'awiya (R.A.A.) wrote a letter, which Hadrat Abu Muslim (R.A.A.) carried to Kufa and delivered it to Hadrat Ali (R.A.A.), who after reading it wrote the following reply:

In the Name of Allah, Most Compassionate, Most Merciful

From the servant of Allah, Ali Amir-ul Momineen to Mu'awiya ibn Abi-Sufyan:

Well now! Khaulani has brought your letter to me. You have written that I deserted Usman (R.A.A.) and instigated people against him. In fact I have done nothing of the sort, except that when people got annoyed with the late Caliph, some withdrew support to him while others assassinated him, while I remained confined to my house and kept myself aloof from his affairs. Now, if you blame me for the uncommitted sin and hide the facts well known to you, then it is your own option.

As regards your demand for handing over to you the assassinators of Usman (R.A.A.), I do not agree with it because I perfectly know your plan to utilise it as a means to fulfil your intentions and designs, with no purpose to revenge the blood of Usman (R.A.A.). By my life, if you do not give up your rebellion and opposition, the same chastisement will be on you, which has fallen over every Tryant, Sinner or Rebel. (Wassalam)

(Akhbar-al-Tiwal, p. 173)

(8)

TO HADRAT MU'AWIYA (R.A.A.)

According to another report Hadrat Ali (R.A.A.) sent the following letter in reply to that letter of Hadrat Mu'awiya (R.A.A.) which was delivered to him by Hadrat Abu-Muslim Khaulani (R.A.A.)

In the Name of Allah, Most Compassionate, Most Merciful

From the servant of Allah, Ali Amir-ul-Momineen to Mu'awiya ibn Abi-Sufyan:

Well now! Khaulani has delivered me your letter. You have mentioned of the reward in the shape of Revelations and true guidance with which Allah, the Almighty blessed Prophet Muhammad (S.A.W.). Undoubtedly Allah is Praiseworthy, Who fulfilled His promise with Muhammad (S.A.W.) (favoured him with success), helped him with His victory and stabilised firmly his position in the country. When the enemies and malicious people fell upon him (The Holy Prophet S.A.W.)., scorned him, united on his vilification, prepared for fighting him out of malice, decided collectively to exile him, his relatives and companions out of country, when most of the Arabs, united in his enmity, prepared for the battle of Ahzab.[1]

He (Allah) helped him till the Will of Allah and the truth prevailed, although the enemies disliked it. When the elders[2] of your tribe were on the fore-front in his opposition, what to speak of the juniors of the tribe, except those whom Allah saved.

---

1. Battle of Ahzab is also known as Battle of Khandaq (Trenches) in which 10,000 people of Quraish and other tribes of Arabia like Ghutfan, Ashja, Banu Saleem and Bani Asad etc. participated. They hatched the plan for the assassination of the Holy Prophet (S.A.W.) and invaded Madinah.
2. Abu-Sufyan (R.A.A.) father of Hadrat Mu'awiya (R.A.A.), then a non-Muslim commanded the combined army of unbelievers.

You have also mentioned that Allah has selected some Muslims for your help and support, thus they have secured their position before Allah in the ranks of Islam. In your view, the Caliph (Abu Bakr Siddiq R.A.A.) and the Caliph of the Caliph Umar Farooq (R.A.A.) were the most outstanding and superior to all others in respect of well-being and obedience to Allah and His Messenger (S.A.W.), I say on oath, undoubtedly their status in Islam is very lofty and (on their death) Islam has sustained a deep wound. May Allah bestow His blessings and reward them the best return for their Deeds.

You have further stated that Usman (R.A.A.) also ranked like them. As such, if Usman (R.A.A.) was pious, he would soon meet his Lord, Who bestows great reward even for small virtue. May Allah multiply his virtues and bestow great recompense. If (he was) a wrong doer, he would soon meet the Lord, All Forgiving, for Whom the forgiving of wrongs is of little importance.

I swear! I hope when Allah will award people in accordance with their service and sanctity to Islam, Allah and His Messenger, the greatest share will be ours, the family of Holy Prophet (S.A.W.), because we, the family members of the Prophet (S.A.W.), have been first to accept the Faith and testify His Prophethood when he invited the people to accept the Faith and believe in Oneness of Allah. Thus in no time we got the exalted and respected position. None of the Arab inhabitants save us worshipped Allah.

Observing this our people conspired to assassinate our Holy Prophet (S.A.W.) and uproot us. Accordingly they hatched deep conspiracies and took many drastic steps (against us). They restrained our movements, withheld our economic activities, exposed us to constant fear and danger, posted spies and guards on us, compelled us to move towards desolate barren mountains, fanned the fire of battle against us and made written agreements between themselves that none should provide us meas nor establish matrimonial relations, nor transact any business with us. Nobody should offer us shelter or protection unless we hand over the Messenger of Allah (S.A.W.) to them for assassination and amputation. We could secure peace during the Hajj days only.[1]

But Allah, the Almighty, bestowed on us the courage to protect and guard the Messenger of Allah (S.A.W) from the danger of those days, defend him, shoot arrows agaisnt enemies to save his honour and draw sword in his support. In this struggle the object of our faithfuls was to gain recompense from Allah only, and those of the infidels, the object was to help their families. In this connection it was clear that among Quraish those who had embraced Islam were safe from atrocities which beset us, because some of them were protected (by their infidel allies) under the previous agreements and other belonged to the tribes which were their protectors. Therefore, they remained safe from the destruction and killings which we suffered. The major succour for us was the Will of Allah.

---

1. When the infidels of Makkah became tired of their numerous attempts of all kinds and did not succeed to suppress the Islamic movement, they decided in a general meeting to make social boycott of Bani Hashim and Bani Muttalib. Consequently Mansoor ibn Ikrama ibn 'Amr ibn Hashim drafted a covenant that no one would establish a matrimonial or any other relation with them, transact any business and maintain friendly association and after signature of all concerned, it was displayed at the Ka'bah. Consequently all Bani Hashim (both Muslims and non-Muslims) gathered at the house of Abu Talib, and moved to Shaib-i-Abi Talib (a valley between two hills). Only Abu Lahab broke off from them and associated with the infidels of Makkah and extended all assistance against his own family. Guards were posted at the valley against Bani Hashim to check their exit from there and the supply of anything to them. This was a great adversity for Bani Hashim as it made their life very hard. They were exposed to numerous physical and mental oppressions. This boycott continued continuously for three years. At last Mut'im ibn 'Adi tore off that covenant and thus Bani Hashim were relieved of that oppression.

(Sirah Ibn Hisham, vol. 1: p. 215)

Then Allah ordained His Prophet (S.A.W.) for migration and thereafter, allowed them to fight against the infidels. During the peak hours of the battles when people wanted to keep themselves safe and the enemy would throw challenge to combat, he (S.A.W.) would advance his family members to meet them. Thus he (S.A.W.) saved his companions from the swords and the spears of the enemy. Consequently Ubaida ibn Haris (R.A.A.) fell martyr in the battle of Badr, Hamza (R.A.A.) in the battle of Uhud, and Ja'far and Zaid (R.A.A.) in the battle of Mauta; and if you like, I might name another person (meaning himself) who, like these martyrs many a time yearned to earn martyrdom while fighting along with the Prophet (S.A.W.) (in battles). But the death hastened in the case of those martyrs and deferred in my case. Their adoption of virtue was due to Allah's Kindness and Favour. Thereafter, I neither heard of nor seen any one who excelled those persons whose name I have given to you. For sincerity and obedience to Allah and His Prophet (S.A.W.) none could match them to face hardship in adversity or prosperity, in battles or other occasions of danger in the company of Holy Prophet (S.A.W.). Mohajireen possess many other outstanding qualities and Allah will compensate for their noble deeds.

It is pity that time has so changed that now that man, who is neither superior to me nor has any seniority (in Islam) over me, which none possesses except me, is rising against me in opposition.

It is, therefore, not strange that any claimant may claim (for anything) not known to me or not in my opinion, in the knowledge of Allah. In all circumstances we must praise Allah.

Then, you have mentioned about my bearing malice against the Caliphs, my late offering of oath of allegiance to them and revolt against them, I seek the refuge of Allah from revolt (I definitely did not commit it). As regards my late approach for oath of allegiance and disapproval of their

Caliphate, it is not necessary for me to offer any apology to people because Allah has already made a decision (on Caliphate) at the time of the passing away of the Holy Prophet (S.A.W.). (That is to say) when the Quraish claimed leadership for their group while the Ansar (local inhabitants of Madinah) for themselves, the latter handed over the Caliphate and government to the emigrants on yielding to their plea that Holy Prophet Muhammad (S.A.W.) belonged to them, therefore, they were more deserving for the leadership. Consequently, when they (emigrants) established their right for Caliphate vis-a-vis Ansar on the basis of their relationship with the Holy Prophet (S.A.W.), then one who would be nearer in relationship with the Prophet (S.A.W.) would be also more deserving for that Caliphate.[1] In the absence of this principle, the Ansar were more rightful to the Caliphate on the basis of their majority. (Now) I fail to understand whether my companions (the emigrants) have been absolved of the charge of snatching my right or have done injustice to Ansar. But nay I have

---

1. There is wide difference on this point between two important sects of Muslims. *Sunnis* say that Islam is a democratic system and there is no room for family succession or heirdom. *Ansar* gave up their claim for Caliphate as they agreed that *Muhajireen* (emigrants) deserved more for Caliphate as they were heralds of believers and first among the Muslims. They also agreed that Hadrat Abu Bakr (R.A.A.), apart from his services and sacrifices for Islam, was the officially nominated one for the Caliphate by the Holy Prophet (S.A.W.) himself. He is the only Muslim, who led the prayers during the life-time of Holy Prophet (S.A.W.) even in his presence. Had the relation with the Holy Prophet (S.A.W.) been the criteria of Çaliphate, Hadrat Usman (R.A.A.) deserved more as he had married two daughters of the Holy Prophet (S.A.W.) while Hadrat Ali (R.A.A.) married only one daughter.

   Moreover, Holy Quran has categorically refused the family relation without the merit of Faith (IMAN) and good deeds. In this respect example of father of Hadrat Ibrahim (A.S.), son of Hadrat Nooh (A.S.), wife of Hadrat Loot (A.S.) and uncle of Holy Prophet (S.A.W.) have been cited repeatedly.

   While *Shias* say that Islamic system is based on family succession and heirship. In this regard they present the claim of Hadrat Ali and his associates.

deduced that my right was snatched and I have abandoned my right in their favour for Allah's Pleasure. May Allah forgive them.

As regards your reference to the matter of Usman (R.A.A.) that I snapped all ties with him and incited the people against him, you have received the news of the acts of Usman (R.A.A.) with the people and you have also seen how the people reacted against him and you know full well that I remained aloof from all those events. Now if you put the blame on me on this issue for an uncommitted sin and hide the facts known to you, it is your option.

Whatever you have written about the assassinators of Usman (R.A.A.), I thought over it deeply, examined it minutely, but I find no point in handing over them (the assassinators) to you or to anyone else.

Behold! Now I swear, if you do not abandon your rebellious ways and disobedience, you will soon come to know those whom you are searching for, and they will not give you trouble of search either on land or water, or mountain or surface of earth (that is my army will itself array against you and you will need not come out). But, (in fact) the success of your search will prove unpleasant to you and the encounter with them will not be delightful for you.

Again your father Abu Sufyan visited me at the time of the demise of the Holy Prophet (S.A.W.) and stressed on my right for succession to the Prophet (S.A.W.) and the government and that he would support me against those who would oppose me. Then he requested me to advance the hand for allegiance, but I did not do so.[1] You are aware of the consent and intention

1. This refers to the incident which took place at the time of Oath of Allegiance in favour of Hadrat Abu Bakr (R.A.A.). It is said that Hadrat Abu-Sufyan (R.A.A.) came to Hadrat Ali (R.A.A.) and enquired why in his presence the Caliphate is being assigned to a junior tribe. He

of your father and also by refusal of the offer for avoiding division between Muslims because people had recently seceded from infidelity (danger of apostasy was imminent). Therefore, (it is confirmed that) your father was better informed about my right than you. As such, if you also recognise my right like your father, you will be among righteous, otherwise, we will seek Allah's help in the fight against you. Allah's peace be on him who deserves.

(Al Iqd-al-Fareed, vol. 2, p. 234)

(9)

TO HADRAT 'AMR IBN AL-'AAS (R.A.A.)

Hadrat 'Amr Ibn al-'Aas (R.A.A.) was one of those who embraced Islam at the time of conquest of Makkah. Egypt was conquered in his command during the Caliphate of Hadrat 'Umar (R.A.A.) who appointed him as the Governor of that province. On this post he continued in the Caliphate of Hadrat Usman (R.A.A.). But after a few years, Hadrat Usman (R.A.A.) dismissed him and appointed his own foster brother Hadrat Abdullah Ibn Sa'd (R.A.A.) as Governor of Egypt in this place. This annoyed Hadrat 'Amr (R.A.A.) and he went back to Madinah. There he started criticising Hadrat Usman (R.A.A.). Occasionally he visited Hadrat Ali (R.A.A.) to instigate him against Hadrat Usman (R.A.A.) to incite them against Hadrat Usman (R.A.A.)

---

requested Hadrat Ali (R.A.A.) to extend his hand for taking oath of allegiance and if people opposed him, he would post a huge contingent of soldiers and horsemen in Madinah for his support. Hadrat Ali (R.A.A.) said: Abu Sufyan, you are always in pursuit of inflicting harm to Islam. Even now you do wish division and bloodshed in Muslims. Go away we do not require counsel and admonition. We have selected Abu Bakr as Caliph finding him most competent.

(Tabari vol. 3, p. 202)

The people of Egypt were not satisfied with Abdullah Ibn Sa'd (R.A.A.). They approached Hadrat Usman (R.A.A.) and lodged their complaint against him. Having been ignored by the Caliph, they grew angry and became his opponent and the situation reached to such a pass that they besieged him. At that time Hadrat 'Amr Ibn al-'Aas left Madinah and went to Palestine. There he got the news of the martyrdom of Hadrat Usman (R.A.A.) and assumption of the office of Caliphate by Hadrat Ali (R.A.A.). He stayed in Palestine for sometime for observing the prevailing situation. When he knew that Hadrat Mu'awiya (R.A.A.) refused to pay allegiance to Hadrat Ali (R.A.A.) and claimed retribtuion for the assassination of Hadrat Usman (R.A.A.), he contacted Hadrat Mu'awiya and entred into an agreement with him that on his success, the governorship of Egypt would be given to him.

While corresponding with Hadrat Mu'awiya (R.A.A.), Hadrat Ali (R.A.A.) also sent this letter to Hadrat 'Amr Ibn al-'Aas (R.A.A.):

In the Name of Allah, Most Compassionate, Most Merciful

From the servant of Allah, Amir-ul Momineen Ali to 'Amr Ibn al-'Aas.

Hereafter: The world attracts (a man) towards itself extracting him from everything and the world-seeker wholly runs after it. The more and more he gains from it, his greediness increases by leaps and bounds and all that is secured does not make him carefree from that not yet gained. Furthermore, man has to leave all his accumulated wealth.

As such only that person is fortunate who derives lesson from the fate of others. Consequently (look)! you shall not destroy your good deeds by collaborating with losing pursuit of Mu'awiya (R.A.A.). He has forsaken the right and opted for the wrong. Wassalam.

(10)

TO HADRAT 'AMR IBN AL-'AAS (R.A.A.)

In the Name of Allah, Most Compassionate, Most Merciful

From the servant of Allah, Ali, Amir-ul Momineen to the [1]breedless 'Amr bin al 'Aas ibn Wail, who, during the period of both ignorance and Islam, were the enemies of the Prophet (S.A.W.) and his family.

Blessing be to the followers of path of righteousness. Hereafter:

You have forsaken your amicable spirit for such a sinner who has been exposed, and he puts blame on the respectables in his meetings and in his sittings, the patient person is called as stupid. Now your heart has become so much subservient to his heart that the famous proverb *'Waafaqa Shannun Tabaqatah,*[2] comes true in your case. Consequently he has deprived you of your faith and trust, your world and Hereafter and everything. Allah is well aware of your state of affairs. As such, now you are like a wolf, who keeps follwoing the lion day in and day out in search of his eaten left-overs and guts of the prey.

But no one is exempted from his fate. (He gets as much as is determined in his destiny). Had you adopted the truth, you would have definitely achieved your object. Undoubtedly one, whose leader is right, definitely gets the right guidance. If Allah invested me with hold on you and on the son of liver-eater mother (Hinda, mother of Hadrat Mu'awiya R.A.A.) I will

---

1. When the son of Holy Prophet (S.A.W.) Hadrat Qasim (R.A.A.) died, the father of Hadrat 'Amr ibn al-'Aas called the Prophet (S.A.W.) as breedless, at which Allah revealed the verse:
   "Lo: it is thy assailant (and not thou) who is without posterity" (S. 108:3): portraying 'Aas as the enemy of Islam, and breedless.
2. It is a proverb spoken on one's complete agreement with anyone.

join you both with those tyrants of Quraish whom Allah has destroyed during the days of Holy Messenger (S.A.W.) and if you could not come under my grip and survived after me, then Allah will decide your fate, and His Revenge and His Punishemnt are enough.

Wassalam

(11)

TO THE PEOPLE OF KUFA

On his way to Basrah, Hadrat Ali (R.A.A.) stayed at a place called Rabzah, near Madinah, and from there he sent Muhammad Ibn Abu Bakr and Mohammad bin Abu Ja'far to Kufa with the following letter addressed to them:

In the Name of Allah, Most Compassionate, Most Merciful

Hereafter: I like you and prefer to stay with you because you loved Allah and His Prophet (S.A.W.). Thus one, who will come to me and render his assistance, he will assist the right and discharge his duty. Wassalam.

(12)

TO THE PEOPLE OF KUFA

According to another report Hadrat Ali (R.A.A.) sent the following letter.

In the Name of Allah, Most Compassionate, Most Merciful

I preferred you over all the cities and made you my ally in every pitfall. Therefore, you should be supporter and helper to the religion of Allah, support me and immediately report to me because I want such reformation so that Ummah of

Muhammad (S.A.W.) should again be united as brothers.

One, who approved and followed it, he approved and followed the Truth, and one who disapproved it he disliked the Truth, treated it ungraceful and despicable. Wassalam.

(13)

TO THE PEOPLE OF KUFA

While on way to Basrah (from Madinah) Hadrat Ali (R.A.A.) sent Muhammad bin Abu Bakr and Muhammad bin Jafar from Rabzah to the people of Kufa with the following letter:

In the Name of Allah, Most Compassionate, Most Merciful

From the servant of Allah, Ali, Amir-ul-Momineen to the Arab Chiefs and Heads of Ansar Families of Kufa.

Hereafter:

I inform you about the affairs of 'Usman (R.A.A.) in such a way that you may believe what you hear as if actually seen. When people put blame on him, I was the only one from the emigrants, who kept him mostly happy and caused him the minimum displeasure. As regards the two (Hadrat Talha and Hadrat Zubair R.A.A.), their mildest disposition was severe and their softest tone was like a roar (that is, they were strong antagonists). On the other side, Hadrat Ayesha (R.A.A.) got also suddenly enraged. Consequently, some persons were stirred up, who assassinated him. Thereafter, people took Oath of Allegiance on my hand without any pressure or aversion, but with their consent and pleasure.

As the Oath of Allegiance was offered in the case of two Caliphs before me, in the same way these two persons (Hadrat

Talha and Hadrat Zubair R.A.A.) offered their Oath of Allegiance to me. Then they sought permission to perform Umra. In fact it was not their aim. Afterwards they withdrew their allegiance to me and became adamant to fight and brought out with them Hadrat Ayesha (R.A.A.) from her house and after choosing people of Basrah for help they proceeded towards that place. Then I chose you for help and have come down to you. I solemnly say I never expect that you will ever prefer anything other than (the Will of) Allah and His Messenger (S.A.W.). Further, I am not fighting with them in my own interest. To seek your aid I am sending my son Hasan, Ammar bin-Yasir and Saad ibn Qais. You will, therefore, prove yourselves worthy of my trust and expectation. None except Allah possesses strength or power....

Wassalam

(14)

TO HADRAT ABU MOOSA ASH'ARI (R.A.A.)

In Rabzah, Hashim ibn 'Utbah met Hadrat Ali (R.A.A.) and informed him of the conversation held between Muhammad bin Abi-Bakr (R.A.A.) and Hadrat Abu Moosa Ash'ari (R.A.A.), Governor of Kufa. After listening to him, Hadrat Ali (R.A.A.) remarked that he had (earlier) wanted to dismiss Hadrat Abu Moosa (R.A.A.) from governorship (but) Ashtar requested me to let him (Abu Musa R.A.A.) to continue. Then Hadrat Ali (R.A.A.) sent back Hashim to Kufa with the follwoing letter addressed to Abu Musa Ash'ari (R.A.A.).

In the Name of Allah, Most Compassionate, Most Merciful

I am sending Hashim ibn Utba to you so as to bring with him the Muslim soldiers under you. Therefore send them towards me as the post which you hold was given to you believing that you will extend cooperation to me in the pursuit of Truth. Wassalam

(Tabari vol. V, p. 198)

HADRAT ABU MOOSA ASH'ARI (R.A.A.)

His name was Abdullah ibn Qais (R.A.A.), and was called Abu Moosa Ash'ari by his family name (Kunniat). He was the inhabitant of Yaman. The Prophet (S.A.W.) had appointed him the Governor of Yaman. (Bukhari, 2:1023).

At the time of martyrdom of Hadrat Umar (R.A.A.) he was Governor of Basrah.

He continued as Governor in the Caliphate of Hadrat Usman (R.A.A.) also. But after six years, Hadrat 'Usman (R.A.A.) removed him and appointed his own maternal cousin Abdullah ibn'Aamir as Governor in his place. Hadrat Abu Moosa (R.A.A.) left Basrah for Kufa after his removal and secluded from public life. When the people of Kufa rebelled against the Governor of Kufa Saeed bin Al 'Aas and requested Hadrat 'Usman (R.A.A.) to appoint Abu Moosa (R.A.A.) as their Governor, he was posted as such in 34 A.H. He held that assignment after the martyrdom of Hadrat 'Usman (R.A.A.) and even some time during the Caliphate of Hadrat 'Ali (R.A.A.). Then he was dismissed by Hadrat 'Ali (R.A.A.).

(Tabari vol. 5, p. 54).

After his dismissal he left Kufa for Makkah. On the issue of arbitration in the battle of Siffin, he was appointed as arbitrator on the persistence of Kufis. He, because of his simplicity, was outwitted by Hadrat 'Amr ibn Al-'Aas (R.A.A.) and lost Hadrat Ali's case. He was extremely sad on that incident and went back to Makkah where he died in 44 A.H.

(Tazkira-tul-Huffaz, vol. 1, p. 21)

(15)

TO HADRAT ABU MOOSA ASH'ARI (R.A.A.)

On receiving letter of Hadrat Ali (R.A.A.) Hadrat Abu Moosa Ash'ari (R.A.A.) summoned Hadrat Sa'eb ibn Malik Ash'ari (R.A.A.) for consultation on issue. Hadrat Sa'eb (R.A.A.) advised him to comply with the orders of Hadrat Ali (R.A.A.). Then Abu Moosa (R.A.A.) said, "But I do not consider it proper." In the meantime, Hadrat Hashim conveyed the news of the meeting and conversation between Abu Moosa (R.A.A.) and Hadrat Sa'eb (R.A.A.) to Hadrat Ali (R.A.A.). Hadrat Ali (R.A.A.) sent Hadrat Hasan (R.A.A.) and Hadrat Ammar bin Yaasir (R.A.A.) to Kufa to enlist the support of the people for re-enforcement. Then he appointed Qaraza ibn Ka'b as Governor of Kufa and sent him to Hadrat Abu Moosa (R.A.A.) with the following letter:

In the Name of Allah, Most Compassionate, Most Merciful

Hereafter:

I think your removal from that government in which Allah has not reserved your share, will not dissuade you to disobey my orders. I have already sent my son Hasan and Ammar ibn Yasir to collect the people for re-enforcement and sending Qaraza ibn Ka'b as Governor-designate of the city. Therefore, you leave with all humiliation my government. If you do not comply with my orders, I have ordered him to fight you. You confront him till he is victorious, he should chop you into pieces.

(Wassalam)

(16)

TO HADRAT TALHA AND HADRAT ZUBAIR (R.A.A.)

When Hadrat Talha and Hadrat Zubair (R.A.A.) proceeded to Basrah with Hadrat Ayesha (R.A.A.), Hadrat Ali (R.A.A.) wrote the following letter to them:

HADRAT TALHA (R.A.A.)

He was one of the vanguards of Islam and among the ten most pious companions of the Prophet (S.A.W.). In the battle of Uhud he defended the Holy Prophet (S.A.W.) when he was surrounded by the infidels. He shielded the Prophet (S.A.W.), took the shower of arrows and spears on his body, and was seriously wounded. After the stoppage of war, the Prophet (S.A.W.) brought him to the camp on his shoulders and gave him the good news of his abode in Paradise.

(Usudul Ghaba, vol. 3, p. 59)

After Hadrat Usman (R.A.A.), Hadrat Talha (R.A.A.) offered allegiance to Hadrat Ali (R.A.A.) on the condition that he would follow the Quran and re-establish the Islamic punishments and Laws. As such Hadrat Talha and Hadrat Zubair (R.A.A.) both demanded the retribution of Hadrat Usman (R.A.A.) from his assassinators which Hadrat Ali (R.A.A.) could not fulfil for some reasons. Thereafter, Hadrat Talha and Hadrat Zubair (R.A.A.) left Makkah with Caliph's permission. There they consulted Hadrat Ayesha (R.A.A.) and marched with an army of 3000 to Basrah. When Hadrat Ali (R.A.A.) got the news, he also marched to Basrah and the Battle of Jamal took palce resulting in excessive bloodshed of pious companions of Holy Prophet (S.A.W.). During the fight

Hadrat Ali (R.A.A.) saw Hadrat Zubair and reminded him of some sayings of the Prophet (S.A.W.). Hadrat Zubair (R.A.A.), on hearing them, withdrew from the fight. Seeing this, Hadrat Talha was also shaken in his determination. Observing this, Marwan ibn Hakam shot a poisonous arrow at him (Hadrat Talha R.A.A.) and he was martyred there.

Hadrat Umar (R.A.A.) had nominated him a member of his Advisory Council. Hadrat Ali (R.A.A.) respected him very much.

In the Name of Allah, Most Compassionate, Most Merciful

Hereafter:

O Talha and Zubair! you are well aware, although you have concealed it that I did not go to people until they themselves approach me and I did not ask for their allegiance until they compelled me to accept their allegiance. Again you both were the first to come forward for taking oath of allegiance to me, without any pressure of fear or temptation. Zubair, you are a famous horseman of Quraish, and Talha you are the leader of emigrants. (You were not in a weak position). Under the circumstances, it was easirer for you to reject allegiance at that very time than your withdrawal of allegiance today. Again the descendants of Usman (R.A.A.) do have the right for claiming retribution (but) you two belong to emigrants. (What connection you have with the case of Usman (R.A.A.)) and (furthermore a serious evil you have committed) that you have brought out your mother (Mother of the Faithful) Hadrat Ayesha (R.A.A.) from the house, where Allah had ordained her to stay. Then Allah is sufficient to account for your doing.

Wassalam

HADRAT ZUBAIR (R.A.A.)

The name of the father of Hadrat Zubair (R.A.A.) was Awwam, and grand-father. Khuwailed. The mother of faithful, Hadrat Khadija (R.A.A.), was the daughter of Khuwailed and paternal aunt of Hadrat Zubair (R.A.A.). His mother, Hadrat Safia (R.A.A.) bint Abdul Muttalib (R.A.A.) was the paternal aunt of the Prophet (S.A.W.) and Hadrat Ali (R.A.A.). Thus Hadrat Ali and Hadrat Zubair (R.A.A.) were related as paternal and maternal cousins. His wife Hadrat Asmaa (R.A.A.) was the daughter of Hadrat Abu Bakr Siddiq (R.A.A.) and thus he was also related with Prophet (S.A.W.) as he (S.A.W.) was husband of his wife's sister. He was one of the ten most pious companions of the Prophet (S.A.W.). He narrated 38 traditions. Hadrat Ali (R.A.A.) reported the Prophet (S.A.W.) saying, "Every messenger had disciples and my disciples are Talha and Zubair (R.A.A.)."

Hadrat Zubair was the first Muslim to draw his sword in the way of Allah. It so happened that once the news broke out that the Prophet (S.A.W.) had been arrested by the infidels of Makkah. Although at that time he was only a young boy, on hearing this news, Hadrat Zubair (R.A.A.) came out with his bare sword and pushing aside the people reached the Holy Ka'ba. There the Prophet (S.A.W.) was standing on the roof of the House. Seeing Zubair in that condition, the Prophet (S.A.W.) enquired, "Zubair, what is the matter?" Hadrat Zubair (R.A.A.) said, "Sir, I got the news of your arrest." On this reply, the Prophet (S.A.W.) gave blessings to him and his sword.

(Usud-ul-Ghaba, vol. 2 p. 196)

Hadrat Zubair (R.A.A.) participated in all battles fought by the Prophet. In the Battle of Jamal (36 A.H. 626 A.D.) when Hadrat Zubair (R.A.A.) confronted Ali (R.A.A.), the latter drew near to him and said, "Zubair, do you remember that the Prophet (S.A.W.) has once said, Zubair, do you hold Ali dear?" Then you had replied in affirmative. Simultaneously the

Prophet (S.A.W.) had also remarked that you would fight with Ali without any casue. Hearing this Hadrat Zubair (R.A.A.) felt ashamed and withdrew from the battle, (*Mustadrak Hakim; vol. 3 p. 266*) and went back to Makkah. He was closely followed by 'Amr ibn Jarmooz. On the way when Hadrat Zubair (R.A.A.) arrived at the valley of As-Saba, he stood to offer his prayers. Finding it a golden opportunity, 'Amir ibn Jamrooz assassinated him during the prayer. As a proof of his killing, he carried Hadrat Zubair's sword and presented it to Hadrat Ali (R.A.A.) for award. Hadrat Ali (R.A.A.) was very much grieved to see the sword. He said this sword of Hadrat Zubair (R:A.A.) was used for defending the Holy Prophet (S.A.W.) from the enemies of Islam. He further said that he heard the Prophet (S.A.W.) saying that the abode of assassinator of Hadrat Zubair (R.A.A.) would be Hell.

MOTHER OF THE FAITHFUL HADRAT AYESHA (R.A.A)

Hadrat Ayesha (R.A.A.) was the daughter of Hadrat Abu Bakr (R.A.A.). Her mother was Zainab with family name of Umm-i-Rooman. She was born four years after the commission of Prophethood and was married to the prophet (S.A.W.) at the age of Ten years. Hadrat Abu Bakr (R.A.A.), while migrating to Madinah with the Prophet (S.A.W.) left his family, including Hadrat Ayesha (R.A.A.) at Makkah. When situation calmed down in Madinah, he sent for his family from Makkah and at the age of 14 years, she was sent as bride to the house of the Holy Prophet (S.A.W.)

Hadrat Ayesha (R.A.A.) passed nine years in the company of the Holy Prophet (S.A.W.). When the Holy Prophet (S.A.W.) passed away, she was of 23 years and survived 48 years after him. She passed away in 58 A.H. at the age of 73 years. According to her wish, she was buried in *Jannat-ul-Baqee*.

The Prophet (S.A.W.) had great love for her and during his last illness, he passed his last days in the apartment of Hadrat Ayesha (R.A.A.) with the consent of other wives. Many events, manifesting his love for Hadrat Ayesha (R.A.A.) have been reported in the books of his traditions and biographies.

In the field of knowledge, she occupied a significant position. She narrated numerous traditions, specially those which related to law and faith (Fiqh). She issued religious verdicts (Fatawa) during the caliphate of Hadrat Abu Bakr, Hadrat 'Umar and Hadrat 'Usman (R.A.A.). Whenever the companions of the Prophet (S.A.W.) faced any difficult problem, it was solved by Hadrat Ayesha (R.A.A.). (Tirmizi). She was also an eloquent orator. She was an expert on commentary of Quran, traditions, intricacies of religious law, eloquence, literature and genealogy.

Hadrat Ayesha (R.A.A.) played a leading role in the battle of Jamal along with Hadrat Talha and Hadrat Zubair (R.A.A.) against Hadrat 'Ali (R.A.A.)

(17)

TO HADRAT AYESHA (R.A.A.)

In the Name of Allah, Most Compassionate, Most Merciful

Hereafter:

You have stepped out of your house for a service from which you are exempted (which was not your responsibility). You, in your view are desirous of reformation of Ummah, please explain what connection women have with forming armies. According to your conception you are demanding the retribution of Usman's blood, although he belongs to Bani Umayya and you come from Bani Taim ibn-i-Murrah. I venture to say on oath that the person who was persuaded you for this venture and has pulled you out of the house is the biggest sinner. As such O Ayesha! Fear Allah, go back to your house and stay behind curtain. Wassalam.

(Al-Imamat wal-Siyasah vol.1, p. 55)

HADRAT QAIS IBN SA'D IBN 'UBADAH (R.A.A.)

Hadrat Qais ibn Sa'ad (R.A.A.) belonged to Khazraj tribe of Madinah and embraced Islam before migration took place. He took part in all the battles fought by the Prophet (S.A.W.) and served as Standard Bearer. He was an important figure during the period of all the four Caliphs (Bukhari 2:1059)

Hadrat Ali posted him as the Governor of Egypt during which time the Egyptians remained under control. In consequence of complaints lodged against him by the Kufis, Hadrat Ali (R.A.A.) removed him from the post and appointed Hadrat Muhammad ibn Abi Bakr (R.A.A.). Then he shifted to Madinah but on Marwan bin Hashim's oppressive treatment, he proceeded to Kufa. (Usud ul Ghabah, 4:216). He participated in the three battles of Jamal, Siffin and Neherwan from Hadrat Ali's (R.A.A.) side. He was a very wealthy man as well as generous. The numerous stories of his generosity are described in history. He extended great help to Muslims and also offered them loans. On the occasion of Jaish ul Khalt he sacrificed so many camels that the government had to hold him from further sacrifice. (Bukhari vol. 3, p-626). He died in 60 A.H.

(18)

TO HADRAT QAIS IBN-I-SA'D (R.A.A.)

Hadrat Ali (R.A.A.) appointed Hadrat Qais ibn-Sa'd (R.A.A.) as Governor of Nadhar.[1] The latter after arrival at Nadhar took Oath of Allegiance from the people but a group refused the allegiance saying to excuse them until the issue of Caliphate is finally decided. In consequence, Hadrat Qais (R.A.A.) despatched a detailed letter to Hadrat Ali (R.A.A.) on the situation. In reply, Hadrat Ali (R.A.A.) sent the following letter:

In the Name of Allah, Most Compassionate, Most Merciful

Hereafter:

Go to those people about whom you have mentioned (in your letter). If they agree to offer allegiance as other Muslims have done, it is good. Otherwise, Allah willing, fight with them. Wassalam (*Tabari vol. 5, p. 230*).

(19)

TO GOVERNOR OF KUFA

Hadrat Ali (R.A.A.) wrote the following letter to the Governor of Kufa after winning the battle of Jamal. The scribe of this letter was Abdullah ibn Rafe' and the messenger Hadrat Zufur ibn Qais (R.A.A.)

In the Name of Allah, Most Compassionate, Most Merciful

Hereafter:

---

1. Nadhar is a town near Kufa.

We fought in the field of Khuraibah[1] in the middle of Jamadi-ul-Aakhir in which Allah awarded them the fate of confronting Muslims (i.e. defeat for the enemies of Muslims). A number of companions of both sides were killed. Our prominent companions who fell martyrs were: Sumama ibn al-Musanna, Hind-ibn-'Amr, 'Ilba-ibn-Haisam and Saihan and Zaid sons of Sohan and Mahdooj.

(Tabari, vol. 5 p.224)

(20)

TO HADRAT MU'AWIYA (R.A.A.)

After taking the oath of Allegiance from the people for his Caliphate and establishing government firmly, Hadrat Mu'awiya (R.A.A.) wrote a letter to Hadrat Ali (R.A.A.). Hadrat Ali (R.A.A.) sent the following reply to that letter:

In the Name of Allah, Most Compassionate, Most Merciful

Hereafter: The significance of the (affairs) of state like that man who keeps his eye not on the army but on his person, and abstains from the absurd talk. I say on oath, if I believe that the strength and help, available to me from the people of Iraq, is more reliable than the strength given to me by Allah, then (in my view) such a believer (himself) has no faith in Allah. Therefore, you ponder over matters like that person whose serious thinking is free from frivolity, because there is no end to such idle talk which has no substance. A man like you, who is the centre of public focus shall not be excused for any fault.

As regards your mention that we and you were a joint force, no doubt we had been so as stated by you. But we were

1. Khuraibah was a vast plain near Kufa.

separated from each other because as Allah sent the Messenger (S.A.W.) from among us and we believed him but you rejected him. Again, your allegation that I killed Talha and Zubair, you were absent from the spot. Had you been present, you would have known the real facts. Therefore, the matter is neither your responsibility (right of interrogation), nor it is necessary for me to present explanation before you. Furthermore your ambition to see me as an Emigrant is baseless as the migration ceased at the time your brother (Yazeed ibn abi Sufyan) was arrested. (There are no migrants among your Companions). Your companions are those people who were granted amnesty by the Prophet (S.A.W.) at the time of conquest to Makkah and according to the verdict of the Prophet (S.A.W.), the migration ceased after the conquest of Makkah. Now if you feel any hurry (to meet) me, abandon it. And if I meet you, it will be proper that Allah may send me to (you) for taking the revenge. Wassalam

(Al Imamat wal-Siyasat, vol. 1, p. 62)

(21)

TO HADRAT MU'AWIYA (R.A.A.)

Ibn-i-Qutaibah reported that while Ali (R.A.A.) was free from the battle of Jamal, and Iraqis offered him their Oath of Allegiance and his government was established, he wrote the following letter to Hadrat Mu'awiya (R.A.A.).

In the Name of Allah, Most Compassionate, Most Merciful

Hereafter:

Behold: Eternal decision and Divine command to be enforced descends from the heaven and falls like rain. The Divine Command invariably prevails. In this matter, neither the pleasure of the creatures has any say nor the willingness of the sons of Adam is required. You would have definitely received the news of assassination of Usman (R.A.A.) May Allah bestow His Belssigns on him) general Oath of Allegiance of the people in my favour, and the attack of oath breakers on me. Therefore, you also do (offer allegiance to me) as all other people have done, otherwise you know me well and are also well aware of my companions. Wassalam

(Al Imamat wal-Siyasat, vol. 1, p. 61)

(22)

TO HADRAT JAREER IBN ABDULLAH AL-BAJALI (R.A.A.)

Hadrat Jareer ibn Abdullah (R.A.A.) belonged to the royal family of Yaman. When he attended the Prophet (S.A.W.) the latter laid his sheet on floor (for sitting) and directed the Muslims to honour when a dignified person came to see you (Asabah 242:1). After the conquest of Mecca he was entrusted the duty of demolishing the Idolatory of Yaman (Ka'aba-i-Yamani). In compliance, he set it on fire and reduced to ashes (*Bukhari-Kitabul Maghazi*). During the Caliphate of Hadrat Umar (R.A.A.) he participated in the battle of Jasarand Yarmook and obtained victory *(Akhbar ul Janah, 119)*. He was posted as governor of Hamdan during the Caliphate of Hadrat Usman (R.A.A.). During the Caliphate of Hadrat Ali (R.A.A.) he went ot Kufa and later to Basrah. At the time of Battle of Jamal he served as messenger of Hadrat Ali (R.A.A.) and proceeded to Hadrat Mu'awiya (R.A.A.). On suspicions of his character on this issue by Maaba Ashter, he was annoyed and went back to Kufa and retired from active life. As such, he did not participated in the Battle of Siffin. He died in 54 A.H. *(Istejaab 91:1)*

In the Name of Allah, Most Compassionate, Most Merciful

Hereafter:

Allah never improves the condition of the people until they strive themselves to improve their own condition. When any harm is intended by Allah to be caused to the people, it cannot be averted and there is none but Allah to protect and help them.

I inform you of my position and of those towards whom we marched on, that is Talha and Zubair (R.A.A.). When these two broke their Oath of Allegiance and misbehaved my governor Usman-ibn-Hunaif, I set off from Madinah along with both emigrants and Asnar. While on way I sent my son Hasan and cousin Abdullah ibn-i-Abbas, 'Ammar ibn Yaasir and Qais ibn Sa'd to Kufa. They requested help from people of Kufa for the sake of Allah and His Messenger (S.A.W.) which they accepted. I marched on to Basrah with all of them and landed in front of the city. I ignored their act of disobedience and asked them to revive their allegiance but they adamantly rejected and agreed to nothing but fighting. (By force of circumstances) I aslo sought Allah's favour against them. Those who survived turned back their faces from me and flew away to the city. Thereafter, they beseeched for the acceptance of the terms for which I had invited them before the flight started. Consequently I preferred peace, and ended the war. Thereafter, I returned to Kura after posting Abudllah ibn-i-Abbas as their governor. I am sending to you Zufur ibn-Qais so that you may enquire from him whatever you desire. Wassalam *(Al Imamat wal-Siyasat vol.1, p. 90)*

(23)

TO HADRAT ASH'AS IBN QAIS KINDI (R.A.A.)

Hadrat Ash'as ibn Qais was an inhabitant of Yaman. He became apostate after the demise of Holy Prophet (S.A.W.).

On invasion of Yaman by Hadrat Abu Bakr (R.A.A.) he was arrested and brought before him. Hadrat Abu Bakr (R.A.A.) asked him "Ash'as, Do you know what I am going to offer you." Hadrat Ash'as replied, "Yes, O leader of the faithful, I know, you will, out of kindness, forgive me and my tribe, set us free, accept my re-conversion to Islam and deliver my wife to me. (He was married to sister of Abu Bakr (R.A.A.) Umme Farwah bint Abu Quhafa during the period of Holy Prophet (S.A.W.); but since he became an apostate after the passing away of Prophet (S.A.W.), his bride was not sent to his home. Thereafter, you will observe that I have proved myself better of all in serving the religion of Allah." Hadrat Abu Bakr (R.A.A.) converted him to Islam, forgave him and set him free and his tribe, and also delivered him his wife, who bore for him three children, Muhammad, Ishaq and Ismail. *(Tabari, vol.3 p. 275)*

Hadrat Ali (R.A.A.) sent the following letter to Hadrat Ash'as Ibn Qais (R.A.A.) through Ziyad ibn Ka'b, who was then the governor of Azerbaijan, and an appointee of Hadrat Usman (R.A.A.)

In the Name of Allah, Most Compassionate, Most Merciful

Hereafter:

Had you not indulged in (some evils) you would have held the top-most position in the government. However, (even now) if you fear Allah, it is possible that the situation may favourably improve. You would have already got the news that people have offered their allegiance to me. Talha and Zubair (R.A.A.) had preceded all others in offering their allegiance to me, but without any casue they have broken it and took the mother of faithful (Hadrat Ayesha R.A.A.) with them to Basrah. Consequently I, in company with Emigrants and Ansar met them and persuaded them to revive their commitments (Allegiance) for which they had gone back, but they did not agree. Then I made utmost efforts in persuasion and continued it with all courtesy and discipline.

(Ash'as behold) your governmental post is not your sweet dish, but given in trust, lying as burden on your shoulders and the entire wealth belongs to Allah. You are its treasurer with my authority until it is given back to me, by the Will of Allah. Also I hope, I shall not prove a bad Caliph for you. Wassalam

(Al Iqd-ul-Farid; vol.2 p. 232)

(24)

TO HADRAT MU'AWIYA (R.A.A.)

When Hadrat Jareer (R.A.A.) went to see Hadrat Ali (R.A.A.) the Caliph said, "Jareer, carry my letter ot Mu'awiya and prove worthy of my opinion about yourself. Behold! On this occasion there are present many companions of Prophet (S.A.W.), emigrants, participants of Badr (Battle) and those next to them, but I choose you from among them for the purpose because the Prophet (S.A.W.) said that Jareer (R.A.A.) is the best of all among the Yamanites. As such it is proper for you to carry my letter to Mu'awiya. If (Mu'awiya) yields to offer allegiance to me like most of the Muslims, it is well and good, otherwise you will convey to him the message of proclamation of war, and further impress upon him that neither I nor people generally agree to his ruling authority." Hadrat Jareer (R.A.A.) said, "I do not feel it reasonable to refrain from service to you, although I do not expect any good for you from Mu'awiya. In future what Allah desires, He will do." The letter is given below:

In the Name of Allah, Most Compassionate, Most Merciful

O Mu'awiya! Although you were in Syria but it was incumbent upon you to offer allegiance to me at Madinah because the same people offered their allegiance to me who had offered their Allegiance to Abu Bakr, Umar and Usman.

This Oath of Allegiance is for the same Caliphate which was previously administered by the previous (Three Caliphs). So who is present has no other choice, and who is absent does not have right of rejection. In fact only Emigrants and Ansar have the right of being members of Advisory Council when they are unanimous on the leadership of certain person and name him, it may be considered as Allah's choice and assent. Any one who turns out of their decision they persuade him to return and submit; but if he refuses, war is waged against him for disagreement with Muslims. Allah will worth his choice and throw him into Hell which is a very bad place. Look Mu'awiya, Talha and Zubair (R.A.A.) first offered their allegiance to me and then broke it. Their act was tantamount to Apostasy. After all-out attempts (to straighten the matter which failed) I had to fight against them in which the right prevailed and Allah's that Order, which they did not like any way, was ultimately enforced (i.e. they were defeated and I emerged victorious and my Caliphate survived).

Therefore, it is proper for you to offer allegiance to me like most of the Muslims because peace is the best thing for you as well as for your companions. On the contrary, you may, on your own accord, invite trouble for yourself. If you choose trouble, I may be forced to attack you and I will seek Allah's help against you.

It has come to my notice that you are propagating too much about Usman's assassination. Behold! first you offer allegiance to me, then come to me along with the people for my decision and I shall award the decision to the parties according to Quran and Sunnah of the Prophet (S.A.W.). As regards your design (retribution of Usman's blood) for which you are adamant, it is like that trick which is adopted for weaning an infant. I am confident if you set aside your desires and use your intellect, you will find me most blameless in the assassination of Usman (R.A.A.). Look Mu'awiya you belong to Tulaqa (persons released on general amnesty at the time of conquest of Makkah) for whom neither Calipahte is lawful nor they can be a leader, nor they have the right to sit in the advisory council. I am sending Jareer (R.A.A.) to you and to your companions. He is a believer and belongs to early emigrants. Therefore even now you offer your allegiance to me and (remember) besides Allah, no one has power. Wassalam

(Al- Imamat wal-Siyasat vol. 1 p. 93)

(25)

TO HADRAT JAREER (R.A.A.)

Hadrat Jareer (R.A.A.) who was sent earlier by Hadrat 'Ali (R.A.A.) as a messenger of his letter to Hadrat Mu'awiya (R.A.A) stayed for three months with him after the delivery of the letter and did not return. Consequently, Hadrat 'Ali (R.A.A.) sent the following letter to him:

In the Name of Allah, Most Compassionate, Most Merciful

May Allah bless you! Hereafter:

No sooner you receive my letter, than persuade Mu'awiya to declare his clear and unequivocal decision and ask him whether he prefers a destructive war or a regretful peace? In case he prefers war, you proclaim the war - Allah does not like the misappropriators - and if he favours peace, take oath of allegiance from him and return to me. Wassalam.

(Al Iqd-ul-Farid, Vol. 2 p. 232).

(26)

TO HADRAT JAREER (R.A.A.)

On receiving the previous letter from Hadrat 'Ali (R.A.A.),Hadrat Mu'awiya (R.A.A.) said to Hadrat Jareer (R.A.A.), "I have a suggestion." Hadrat Jareer (R.A.A.) asked, "What is that?" Hadrat Mu'awiya (R.A.A.) said, "I am writing to 'Ali that he may hand over Egypt and Syria to me and after his death, he may not put on my shoulder the burden of allegiance to anyone else and (in exchange) I will entrust the government to him and recognize his caliphate." Hadrat Jareer (R.A.A.) said, "You may write whatever you wish." In fact, Hadrat Mu'awiya (R.A.A.) intended to abstain from offering allegiance to Hadrat 'Ali (R.A.A.) by demanding Egypt and Syria and get rid of himself from the intricate situation, to which others have succumbed. Accordingly, Hadrat Mu'awiya (R.A.A.) wrote to Hadrat 'Ali (R.A.A.) on the said lines. On receiving the letter of Hadrat Mu'awiya (R.A.A.) Hadrat Ali (R.A.A.) perceived the trap of the former and, therefore, he wrote to Hadrat Jareer (R.A.A.) the following letter:

In the Name of Allah, Most Compassionate, Most Merciful

Hereafter:

The object of Mu'awiya by demanding Egypt and Syria, is to keep him away from the allegiance to me and have a free hand in his activities. Furthermore, he apparently intends to oppress you (by procrastination) and cause delay until he tests (loyalty of) the people of Egypt and Syria. When I was in Madinah, Mughirah ibn Sho'bah had advised me on this issue, recommending me to let Mu'awiya continue as governor of Syria but I had refused to listen him. Allah may not bring me to such a pass in furture that I may accept the misled as my ally. As such, if Mu'awiya offers you allegiance, then well and good, otherwise you come back. Wassalam.

(Al Imamat-wal-Siyasat, Vol. 1 p. 95).

(27)

TO HADRAT ABDULLAH IBN ABBAS (R.A.A.)

Hadrat Abdullah Ibn Abbas (R.A.A.) ibn Abdul Muttalib was an illustrious companion and cousin of the Holy Prophet (S.A.W.). He was born in Makkah and remained in the company of the Holy Prophet (S.A.W.) till his death. He was a commentator of Quran and narrator of traditions. He has narrated 1660 true traditions. He participated from Hadrat 'Ali's (R.A.A.) side in the battles of Jamal and Siffin. In his last days, when he lost his eye-sight, he settled in Basrah and passed a secluded life. He died in 88 A.H./687 A.D.:

In the Name of Allah, Most Compassionate, Most Merciful

Behold! Basrah is a landing place for Satan and a thatchery for mischief and disturbances. Therefore, you treat the residents of Basrah with courtesy and remove fear and doubts from their hearts. I have got the news of your wrathful and harsh treatment meted to Bani Tameem. Look! Banu Tameem are those people who, before the setting of one of their stars, have a rising star. They never hasted in waging a war either in the days of ignorance or after the advent of Islam. (Again), they bear close connection and near relationship with us. We will be awarded recompense for giving generous treatment to them and earn sin in throwing them away. Therefore, O son of Abbas! Allah be kind to you, take precautions in commitment of good and evil deeds from your tongue and hands, because we both jointly shoulder the responsibility. You mould yourself according to my thinking and do not let my opinion about yourself be proved incorrect. Wassalam. *(Kitab-al-Siffin. p. 57)*

(28)

TO ZIYAD AND SHURAIH

Hadrat 'Ali (R.A.A.) had sent in the command of Ziyad ibn Nadhar a contingent to 12000 fighters on the occasion of the Battle of Siffin. He belonged to Banu Harith and was an efficient commander.

Shuraih ibn Hani ibn Yazeed al-Harsi al-Muzhaja al-Yemeni al-Kufi was an eminent contemporary of the companions of the Holy Prophet (S.A.W.). Hadrat 'Umar (R.A.A.) had posted him as the judge of Kufa, which post he held continuously for 75 years. Qasim ibn al Mukhirah had reported that he had not seen any Harisi better than him. He was the officer of the military contingent which was sent with the two Arbitrators to Daumat-ul-Jandal on the occasion of Battle of Siffin. He was martyred in 78 A.H./607 A.D. in Sajistan.

When Hadrat 'Ali (R.A.A.) arrived at the bank of river Euphrates, he summoned Ziad ibn Nadhar and Shuraih ibn Hani. They called on him in the condition in which they had left Kufa. They were immediately sent by Hadrat 'Ali toward Mu'awiya (R.A.A.). They departed from Kufa and went along the bank of River Euphrates on which Kufa is situated (i.e. they marched along the bank of the river). When they reached Anat, they got the reports that Hadrat Mu'awiya (R.A.A.) commanding the army of Syria had proceeded from Damascus to fight against Hadrat 'Ali (R.A.A.). They both, after consultation, decided inadvisable to combat with Mu'awiya's army with their small contingent. Consequently, they turned back from there to Hadrat Ali (R.A.A.) and informed him of the position. Hadrat 'Ali (R.A.A.) lauded them and said, "You have done well."

Thereafter, Hadrat 'Ali marched ahead and after crossing the river Euphrates, again sent both of them towards Mu'awiya (R.A.A.). When they arrived near Roman border, they met Abul Aa'war Al Sulami with a contingent of Syrian soldiers. Then they despatched a letter to Hadrat 'Ali (R.A.A.), who sent the following reply to their letter:

In the Name of Allah, Most Compassionate, Most Merciful

I appoint Maalik as your leader: you obey him and carry out his orders because he is a person from whom there is neither the risk of committing a sin nor a lapse, nor of tardiness on the occasion demanding swiftness not even swiftness on the situation demanding tardiness. I have also ordered him as I have done to you, that before meeting the people (enemy), invite them (to offer allegiance) and exert all possible efforts in that respect, he should not start war against them. Wassalam.

(Tabari, vol. 5, p. 238)

(29)

TO THE PEOPLE OF MERV

When the chief of Merv, Mah'vaih came to Hadrat 'Ali (R.A.A.) for peace and reconciliation, the latter wrote the following letter to the villagers of Merv and Asavirah, army of Salareen and Merv:

In the Name of Allah, Most Compassionate, Most Merciful

Allah's peace be on those who are on the right path.

Hereafter: The headman of Mah'vaih Merv came to me. I am satisfied with him. Wassalam.

(*Tabari, vol. 5 p. 233*).

(30)

TO HADRAT MU'AWIYA (R.A.A.)

In reply to a letter from Hadrat Mu'awiya (R.A.A.) Hadrat 'Ali wrote the following letter in verses:

In the Name of Allah, Most Compassionate, Most Merciful

Hereafter:

I write to you the same which Mukhariq presented, in the form of verses to Bani Falij:

Verse 1 & 2: O horseman! if you meet Bani Falij, wherever they may be, you convey to them the message to meet us and accept our suggestion and come out to us.

(Your state) should not be like that of barren land which is devoid of even earth.

Verse 3: We know Sulaim ibn Mansur that he is highly respectable person; but such a land is in his possession which abounds abundantly by wild animals (which feed themselves upon the leftover prey). Wassalam.

(Akhbar Al-Tiwal,p. 97)

(31)

TO HADRAT MU'AWIYA (R.A.A.)

Hadrat 'Ali sent the following letter in reply to one sent by Hadrat Mu'awiya (R.A.A.):

In the Name of Allah, Most Compassionate, Most Merciful

Hereafter:

I have received a letter from your side from such a person who does not possess his own eyes to guide him nor had a guide to shown him the way. Lust allured him and he succumbed, when it dragged him, he gave in. Mu'awiya! Do you believe that my fault regarding 'Usman's case has made you to hold back your offer of allegiance to me? In fact, by my soul! I am a person from the emigrants— wherever they went I followed, where they reached I also reached, and Allah will neither let them (emigrants) agree on digression nor vanish their sight. Neither have I issued an order which may involve me in the crime of assassination of 'Usman nor have I myself assassinated him, for which retribution be binding on me.

As regards your claim that Syrians have authority on people, please show me only one person out of Syrians belonging to Quraish, who is eligible to speak in the Advisory Council or who is fit for the office of Caliph. If you name any one, then both emigrants and Ansar will refute you. On the other hand I may present so many such persons from among the Quraish of Hijaz. As regards your demand to hand over the assassinators of 'Usman to you, what relation you have with 'Usman. You belong to Bani Umayyah; comparatively, the descendants of 'Usman deserve it more. And if you suppose that you deserve more, then in the first place offer you obedience to me and then bring the people before me for a decision in the matter. So far as the issue of distinction between Basrah and Syria and affairs of Talha and Zubair are concerned, I swear on my soul that there is only one word and that is the general offer of allegiance (to me) - which can neither be revised nor vests in any one under any other kind of authority. As regards your exaggeration about the case of 'Usman, I say on oath that neither it is based on your self conviction nor on any trustworthy news. Had your strength to obliterate my superiority in Islam, relationship with the Prophet (S.A.W.) and nobility of Quraish, I swear on my soul, you would have already done so long ago. Wassalam.

(Al Iqd-ul-Farid, vol.2 p. 283)

(32)

TO HADRAT MU'AWIYA (R.A.A.)

In the Name of Allah, Most Compassionate, Most Merciful

From the servant of Allah, 'Ali, leader of the Faithful, to Mu'awiya ibn Abu Sufyan.

Hereafter:

Behold! This world is a market place and its profit and loss lies in the world Hereafter. Consequently, that perosn is fortunate who contains virtuous deeds as his Capital and who has observed the world in the worldly perspective and evaluated it according to its worth. Behold! In spite of possessing information about you which will not be negated and will reach to its result, I wish to admonish you because Allah has ordained the learned to restore the trust (right) and advise (both) who are on right path and who are digressed. Therefore, you fear Allah and do not be among those people who do not pin their hope in Allah for awarding greatness and for whom punishment has been decided. However, Allah is lying in ambush for you; your world is about to turn back from you and you will have to retreat in grief. Look! In old age, the digression (from truth) and the disobedience which has developed in your person; give it up because your position is like that worn out cloth which if mended on one side, rends on the other.

Having deceived from your disobedience, you got killed many people and offered them to the waves of river (of disobedience), and darkness has spread over them and dashing waves of deluge of uncertainty are battering them and turned back faces; they have retreated; and they have turned their back and have sought the help of their families, except those sharp-sighted persons who abandoned you because when you burdened them with heavy load and tried to further misguide them they understood you and instead of extending you cooperation, rushed towards Allah. Therefore, O Mu'aiya! You fear Allah about yourself and get your person out of Satan's command because the world is soon to abondon you and the world Hereafter is nearer to you. Wassalam. (*Sharh Ibn-al-Hadeed, vol. 2, p. 281)*

(33)

TO HADRAT MU'AWIYA (R.A.A.)

The previous letter when delivered to Hadrat Mu'awiya (R.A.A.), he sent a reply to Hadrat 'Ali. The following letter was dictated to Hadrat Abdullah Ibn Rafe (R.A.A.) in reply to that letter:

In the Name of Allah, Most Compassionate, Most Merciful

Hereafter:

I received you letter. You have written if we both had realized that the war between us would come to such a pitch, we would not have dared (to involve) each other. In this connection, you may note that subsequently we will continue indulgence in it (war) to the utmost end to which (the war) has not reached.

As regards your demand for Syria, which I have already refused to secede to you, I cannot offer you now in any way. So far as the hope and terror of competion between me and you is concerned, even your suspicion for your success is not as much deep, as I am confident (of my success). The Syrians are not as much greedy of this world as the people of Iraq are for the Hereafter.

Regarding your claim that we both are descendants of Abd Manaf, yes, we both are so. But neither Umayya was euqal to Hashim, nor Harb to Abdul Muttalib, nor Abu Sufyan to Abu Talib. Not even emigrants and Tulaqah (persons released on amnesty after the conquest of Makkah). Do supporters of truth and transgressors bear any relation? (Instead) we have the honour of Prophethood (on our side), for which we killed many great and renowned (infidels) and made the free (infidels) as slave and sold them. Wassalam.

(Al Imamat wal-Siyasat, p. 114)

(34)

TO HADRAT MU'AWIYA (R.A.A.)

In the Name of Allah, Most Compassionate, Most Merciful

From the servant of Allah, 'Ali, leader of the Faithful, to Mu'awiya ibn Abu Sufyan.

Hereafter:

Look, the best task for a man is to strive for that thing which may sanctify his deeds, be source of excellence and save him from evil. Rebellion and falsehood demean man both in this world and the Hereafter and expose his ills before a fault-finder. Look shun this world because whatever you obtain from it, is not matter of gratification. You know full well that whatever is destined for you to lose, you cannot get it. Beyond doubt, people aspired for an improper act (for which) they misinterpreted (the words of) Allah and, in return, Allah belied them and gave them a little (worldly) gain and then awarded them the severe torment in the Hereafter. So, fear of that day when that man will be happy whose end has been good and that man will be repentant who allowed the Satan upper hand over (him), accepted his leadership; did not resist him, trapped in the deception of the world, was satisfied with him.

You are calling me towards the decision of the Quran.

I know very well that neither you are follower of Quran, nor (following) its decision is your aim. In fact, Allah Alone is Competent for providing help. We do not accept your invitation but accept the Quran and its decisions and one who is not contented with the verdict of Quran is grossly misled. Wassalam.

(Sharh Ibn Abi-al-Hadeed, vol. 1, p. 188)

(35)

TO KHARIJIS[1]

After Kharijis rose in rebellion against Hadrat Ali (R.A.A.) and Hadrat Abu Musa left for Makkah, Hadrat Ali sent back Hadrat Ibn-e-Abbas (R.A.A.) to Basrah. He first delivered a sermon in Kufa and then he wrote the

---

1. In the beginning, the Kharijis were the staunch supporters of Hadrat Ali (R.A.A.). They fought bravely and valiantly as the soldiers of Hadrat Ali's force against Hadrat Mu'awiya (R.A.A.). When Hadrat Ali (R.A.A.) agreed for arbitration by Quran, in the battle of Siffin fought against Hadrat Mu'awiya, the Kharijis became most ferocious opponents of not only Hadrat Ali (R.A.A.) but also Hadrat Mu'awiya and Hadrat 'Amr bin al'Aas who was one of the arbitrators. They decided to assassinate all these three leaders at an appointed date and time. Fortunately they could not find Hadrat Mu'awiya and Amr bin al'Aas. But unfortunately they found Hadrat Ali (R.A.A.) leading Morning prayers in the Mosque.They attacked him fatally and this shining sun of knowledge and character set forever.

following letter to Kharijis:

In the Name of Allah, Most Compassionate, Most Merciful

From the servant of Allah, (Leader of the faithful) to Yazid ibn Husain, Abdullah ibn Wahab-ar-Rasi and their companions.

Hereafter:

The two erroneous members (for the Arbitration Committee) on whose verdict I had agreed to assent, have delivered (theri verdict) against the Book of Allah, and followed their lust against the guidance of Allah. Therefore, they have neither acted on Sunnah nor followed the injunctions of the Holy Quran. So, Allah, His Messenger and the Muslims in general are exonerated from their verdict. It is proper for you that as soon as you receive my this letter, start towards me because I am ready to march on your and my enemy, and we still stick to that point which we had decided before. Wassalam.

(Tabari, vol. 6, p. 44)

(36)

TO HADRAT ABDULLAH IBN ABBAS (R.A.A.)

When Hadrat 'Ali (R.A.A.) made a stay at Nukhailah and he read the reply of Kharijis, he was disappointed from them. He proceeded to Syria and sent the following letter to Abdullah Ibn Abbas (R.A.A.) through 'Utba ibn Akhnas, a man of Banu Sa'ad ibn Bakar tribe:

In the Name of Allah, Most Compassionate, Most Merciful

Hereafter:

I have come out from my camp at Nukhaila and have determined to march on to our Syrian enemy. Therefore, you, by the time my message reaches you, get people prepared and ready, and stay there till my further orders reach you. Wassalam.

(Tabari, vol. 6, p. 44)

(37)

TO SA'D IBN MASUD SAQAFI (R.A.A.)

Hadrat Sa'ad ibn Masud Saqafi (R.A.A.) was the governor of Madinah, appointed by Hadrat 'Ali (R.A.A.) and continued on that post till the period of Hadrat Hasan (R.A.A.). When Hadrat Hasan (R.A.A.) was wounded in Madain, Hadrat Sa'ad remained in his attendance and treated him.

Hadrat 'Ali (R.A.A.) wrote the following letter to Hadrat Sa'ad ibn Masud Saqafi (R.A.A.):

In the Name of Allah, Most Compassionate, Most Merciful

Hereafter:

I am sending Ziyad ibn Khasafa to you, therefore send with him the all experience Kufi soldiers which are available with you; hasten it if Allah so wills! and none except Allah has any power.

(Tabari, vol. 6, p. 45)

(38)

TO HADRAT ABU MUSA ASH'ARI (R.A.A.)

When Hadrat Abu Musa Ash'ari (R.A.A.) arrived at Makkah from Dauma-tul-Jandal,[1] he received letters from Hadrat Mu'awiya (R.A.A.) and Hadrat 'Amr ibn al 'Aas (R.A.A.). On getting this news, Hadrat Ali (R.A.A.) felt sorry for him and desired to win him over again. Consequently, he wrote the following letter:

In the Name of Allah, Most Compassionate, Most Merciful

Hereafter:

You are that man whom the human lust has digressed and deception has overpowered. (Look!) You beseech for Allah's forgiveness and He will pardon you because one who seeks His forgiveness, is pardoned by Him. Indeed, He bestows His forgiveness and does no discriminate (in His Forgiveness) and He likes more His those servants, who fear Him. Wassalam.

(Al Imamat-wal-Siyasat, vol. 1 p. 133)

---

1. In the Battle of Siffin, Hadrat Abu Musa Ash'ari (R.A.A.) from Hadrat Ali's (R.A.A.) and Hadrat 'Amr ibn al'Aas (R.A.A.) from Mu'awiya's (R.A.A.) side were nominated as members of the Arbitration Committee and Daumatul-Jandal was decided to be the venue for meeting. In that meeting Hadrat Abu Musa (R.A.A.) was defeated politically by Hadrat 'Amr Ibn al Aas (R.A.A.). Hadrat Abu Musa Ash'ari was so much ashamed of this defeat, that he proceeded directly to Makkah from Daumat-ul-Jandal.
   Daumat-ul-Jandal is that portion of Iran where the Holy Prophet (S.A.W.) had sent Hadrat Khalid bin Walid (R.A.A.) as the commander of the army. The people of that area had remained neutral in conflict between Hadrat 'Ali and Hadrat Mu'awiya (R.A.A.).

(39)

TO MAALIK IBN HARIS ASHTAR (R.A.A.)

Hadrat Maalik ibn Haris Ashtar (R.A.A.) was master of military tactics and a valiant commander of the army of Hadrat 'Ali (R.A.A.). He always kept his bow ready in his hands. When Kharijis assaulted Hadrat Muhammad ibn Abi Bakr, Hadrat 'Ali posted Ashtar as the governor of Egypt and sent him there with an army at his command. On the other side when Hadrat Mu'awiya (R.A.A.) came to know that Ashtar was coming in place of Hadrat Muhammad Ibn Abi Bakr, he realized that to handle Muhammad ibn Abi Bakr was easier, but Ashtar would prove a very hard opponent. Therefore, he wrote the chief of 'Areesh for his cooperation to kill Maalik Ashtar. For this service, he offered him to write off the remaining tax due to him. The chief fell victim to the temptation and when Ashtar reached his village, he offered poisoned honey to him which killed him. When news of the death of Ashtar reached Hadrat Mu'awiya (R.A.A.), he remarked that honey is also one of the forces of Allah.

After the Battle of Siffin, when the affairs of the government were normalised, Hadrat 'Ali (R.A.A.) wrote the following letter to Maalik Ashtar, who was then in Naseebain:

In the Name of Allah, Most Compassionate, Most Merciful

Hereafter:

You are definitely among those people whose help I seek for the establishment of the religion, to pull the pride of the sinners and re-enforce the hazardous boundaries. I had appointed Muhammad ibn Abi Bakr (R.A.A.) as the governor of Egypt. The Kharijis assaulted him there. Since he is a young youth, who has little experience of war and other affaris, it is therefore proper for you to come to me immediately so that we may think over some suitable plan; and appoint a reliable, trustworthy man from among your friends to officiate you in your absence. Wassalam.

(Tabari, vol. 6, p. 54).

(40)

TO MUHAMMAD IBN ABI BAKR (R.A.A.)

His mother was Hadrat Asmaa bint 'Umai al-Khasamiah, who was the sister of Umm-ul-Momineen Hadrat Maimoonah (R.A.A.), the pious wife of the Holy Prophet (S.A.W.). Hadrat Asmaa was first married to Hadrat Ja'far (R.A.A.) ibn Abi Talib and Muhammad ibn Jafar was born. After Hadrat Ja'far's martyrdom, Hadrat Abu Bakr (R.A.A.) married Asmaa Bint Umai and Hadrat Muhammad ibn Abi Bakr was born. After Hadrat Abu Bakr's death, Hadrat 'Ali (R.A.A.) married her. At that time, Hadrat Muhammad ibn Abi Bakr was very young. Hadrat 'Ali (R.A.A.) brought him up like his own son and called him also as such. When Hadrat 'Ali posted him as governor of Egypt, he was an inexperienced and young warrior and therefore the people of Khurabitah started fighting with him. On the otherside, Hadrat Mu'awiya (R.A.A.) sent a powerful army under the command of Hadrat 'Amr ibn al-Aas (R.A.A.) for the aid of the people of Khurabitah. Hadrat Muhammad ibn Abi Bakr (R.A.A.) could not successfully check that huge army and he was martyred in 38 A.H.

When Muhammad ibn Abi Bark (R.A.A.) got the news that Hadrat 'Ali (R.A.A.) had sent Maalik Ashtar (as governor to replace him), he was displeased. On receiving the information that the posting of Maalik Ashtar caused displeasure to Hadrat Muhammad ibn Abi Bakr (R.A.A.), he wrote the following letter to him:

In the Name of Allah, Most Compassionate, Most Merciful

Hereafter:

I have received the information of your displeasure and anger on posting Maalik Ashtar in your place. (Look!) I have not done so that I consider you lacking in fighting or I want to check you myself in your unjust efforts. If I had withdrawn you from the present assignment (for some reasons), I would have entrusted you another assignment, which may have been easier than this for you and more pleasing with regard to authority. The person whom I had appointed as the governor of Egypt was our well-wisher and taught for enemies (but alas!) his days were numbered and he met his death. I am pleased with him and may Allah also bestow him double recompense and provide him a better last resort.

(Now it is proper for you) to put a bold front against your enemies and be ready for fighting and call (the people) to the path of your Lord with wisdom and fair exhortation. (Look!) remember Allah exclusively, beseech for His extensive help and fear Him intensely. He will suffice you in your important affairs and assist you in the government. Allah may help me and you in those affairs which we can't perform without His blessings. Wassalam.

(Tabari, vol. 6, p. 56).

(41)

TO THE PEOPLE OF EGYPT

The freed slave of Ashtar related that after Ashtar's death the following letter of Hadrat Ali (R.A.A.) was found in his luggage for the people of Egypt:

In the Name of Allah, Most Compassionate, Most Merciful

From the servant of Allah, 'Ali, leader of the faithful to that group of Muslims who were enraged, when the disobedience of Allah had started in the country and tyranny had overcast over all good and bad, neither truth was being practised nor evil was being refrained. Allah's blessings be on you and I offer praise to Allah, who is only, beside Whom there is no God.

Hereafter:

I have sent towards you a servant of Allah who does not sleep in time of danger and does not turn his face from enemies for fear of calamities; he is more terrible than the burning fire for the unbelievers; he is Maalik ibn Haris Mazhaji. You listen to him and obey his orders because he is one of the swords of Allah, the cut of which neither lessens nor blunts. If he sends you forward, go forward, and if he disperses you, scatter yourselves, because, without my order, he neither advances nor retreats. Sending him to you, I have given you preference on my own self, because he is very hard for your enemies. May Allah protect you through His guidance and keep you steadfast on your belief. Wassalam.

(Tabari. vol. 6, p. 55).

(42)

TO MUHAMMAD IBN ABI BAKR (R.A.A.)

On receipt of the letter of Hadrat 'Amr and Hadrat Mu'awiya (R.A.A.) addressed to him, Hadrat Muhammad ibn Abi Bakr (R.A.A.) put them in an envelope, enclosed his own letter also and sent them to Hadrat 'Ali (R.A.A.). In his letter he informed Hadrat 'Ali (R.A.A.) about the gathering of people around Hadrat 'Amr ibn al-'Aas (R.A.A.) on the border of Egypt and seeking military and economic help from them. Hadrat 'Ali (R.A.A.) sent the following letter in his reply:

In the Name of Allah, Most Compassionate, Most Merciful

Hereafter:

I received your letter. You have written that Amr ibn al-Aas (R.A.A.) has landed with a huge army at the border of Egypt, and his co-thinkers have joined him. (In my view) the joining of supporters of Amr with him is better than their stay with you. Further, you have written that you find some of your companions as cowards in war; however, you do not be coward although they may show cowardice. You fortify your city, keep together your companions and solicit help from Kanana ibn Bishr, who is famous for his loyalty, gentleness and bravery. I am sending you reinforcement to meet the situation, be it hard or easy. Put a bold front against the enemy, apply your intellect and insight and wage war with them according to your intelligence and prudence. Fight firmly with the intention of gaining recompense from Allah even if your number is small, because Allah sometimes dignifies the small group and disgraces the majority.

I have read the letters of sinner son of sinner, Mu'awiya and the sinner, son of the infidel 'Amr; both are united in sinful acts, unanimous in government affairs, offerers of bribe and disliked (throughout) the world. They have obtained their shares of worldly benefit as the people before them have obtained their worldly benefits. Their thundering and flash may not frighten you. If you have not already given them replies, then you give them the reply which they deserve, as you can write them as you wish. Wassalam

(Tabari, vol. 6, p. 58).

(43)

TO HADRAT ABDULLAH IBN 'ABBAS (R.A.A.)

When Hadrat Muhammad Ibn Abu Bakr fell martyred and the news reached Hadrat 'Ali (R.A.A.) he was deeply seized with sadness and signs of grief and sorrow appeared on his face. Standing among the people he delivered a speech and thereafter sent the following letter to Hadrat Abdullah ibn Abbas (R.A.A.), who was then in Basrah.

In the Name of Allah, Most Compassionate, Most Merciful

This letter of servant of Allah, 'Ali, leader of the faithful is addressed to Abdullah ibn Abbas, Assalam-o-Alaikum (Be peace on you): I offer praise and Eulogy to Allah besides whom none is God.

Hereafter:

Egypt has been conquered by enemies and Muhammad ibn Abu Bakr has been martyred. We pray Allah to bestow His Reward and Recompense on him, and we make him provision for ourselves. From the beginning I stayed among the people and before this terrible incident, I had instructed and invited them time and again both openly and privately (for the purpose). But some people did come unwillingly, some made lame excuses and others forsook. I beseech Allah to get me rid of them and give me relief from them at the earliest. By Allah, had I no temptation of martyrdom while fighting with enemy, I would not have liked to live with them for a single day. May Allah keep us firmly on the right path and favour us with His fear and guidance. Beyond doubt He is Omnipotent. Wassalam.

(Tabari, vol. 6, p. 68).

(44)

TO ZIYAD IBN UBAID

Hadrat 'Ali (R.A.A.) sent A'yan ibn Zubai'ah al-Mujashe'i to Basrah and wrote the following letter to Ziyad:

In the Name of Allah, Most Compassionate, Most Merciful

From the servant of Allah, the leader of the Faithful, 'Ali, to Ziyad ibn 'Ubaid.

Allah's Peace be on you.

Hereafter:

I am sending A'yan ibn Zubai'ah to turn his community against Ibn-i-Haz'rami. Therefore, you keep an eye on his actions and if he does (so) and makes utmost effort and by this effort these vagabonds disperse, this is what I want. And if by this (effort) the disobedience and opposition of people grows further, then send one of your followers towards the disobedients to wage a war against them. If it so happens, and I hope it will, (then this is what I want) and if you find slackness in your supporters and fear that what you wish may not take place, then prolong the matters and use delaying tactics. Soon after, you will see that the army of Muslims has reached you and Allah will destroy those cruel rioters and help Muslims. Wassalam.

(Sharah Ibn Abul-Hadeed, vol. 1, p. 353).

(45)

TO HIS GOVERNORS

When Khirrit ibn Rashid, with three hundred people of Najiah tribe revolted and left Kufa, Ziyad ibn Khasafah requested Hadrat 'Ali (R.A.A.) to allow him to follow them so that he could bring them back to him. Hadrat 'Ali (R.A.A.) enquired, "Do you know to which direction they have gone?"

Ziyad replied, "No sir! I will go out of the city and shall enquire from the people about them and follow them on their footprints." Hearing this, Hadrat 'Ali (R.A.A.) said, "Well! you may go; may Allah protect you and be kind; but look! when you reach Der-Abi Musa, you stay there and do not go ahead without my orders. If they have gone openly as a group, my governors will write to me about them, and if they have gone stealthily, then this matter will be more concealed from them (governors); and soon I will write to the governors about them." Thereafter, Hadrat 'Ali (R.A.A.) issued the following orders to his governors:

In the Name of Allah, Most Compassionate, Most Merciful

Hereafter:

Some people have fled away from here and I presume, they have gone towards Basrah. Therefore, you make enquiries about them from the people of your area and spread your spies after them on all sides of your state and whatever information you get about them, send in writing to me. Wassalam.

(Tabari; vol. 6, p. 76).

(46)

TO QARAZAH IBN KA'B (R.A.A.)

After reading the letter of Qarazah ibn K'ab Ansari (R.A.A.) brought by Faij, Hadrat 'Ali (R.A.A.) the leader of Faithful, sent the following reply:

In the Name of Allah, Most Beneficent, Most Merciful

The party, about which you have mentioned, passed by you (unchecked) and martyred a gentle Muslim and our opponents and disobedients took shelter with them. I know, they are the people who have been intoxicated by Satan and thus became misled.

They are like those people who thing that there is no trial (in the world) and thus they have become blind and deaf. (Neither they are capable of hearing the truth nor seeing the right path). They will attentively hear and see on that day when they will be informed of their deeds. You remain steadfast on your duty and keep on receiving your tribute because according to you, you are an obedient and loyal man. Wassalam.

(Tabari, vol. 6, p. 68).

(47)

IN REPLY TO HADRAT AQEEL'S LETTER

In the Name of Allah, Most Compassionate, Most Merciful

From the servant of Allah, the leader of the Muslims, 'Ali, to 'Aqeel ibn Abi Talib.

Allah's peace be on you. I praise and eulogize before you that there is no God save Him.

Hereafter:

Allah may keep you and me in His protection as He protects those who fear without seeing Him. Undoubtedly, Allah is worthy of all praises and is Great and Superior.

Abdul Rehman ibn 'Ubaid came to me with your letter, in which you have written that you have met Abdullah ibn Sa'ad ibn Abi Sarah, while he has been proceeding towards west from Qudaid along with forty youths of the discendants of Tulaqa (people granted amnesty after the Conquest of Makkah). Ibn Sarah is one who has been deceiving, from long time, Allah, His Messenger and His Book. He has abandoned the path of Allah and by his perverseness has risen in revolt (even at the time of Conquest of Makkah, he was among the rebels and apostates). Therefore, you expel from your heart the thought of Ibn Sarah and Quraish and leave them wandering in their perversion, absorbed in revolt and striving strenuously in the barren place, because Quraish have today united to fight with your brother (myself) as they had done before in their war with the Holy Prophet (S.A.W.). They are so much changed as if they are ignorant of his right and rejected his superiority. They cheated him for the sake of their enmity; set up war against him and made all out efforts in their combat with him. They brought the fighting contingents of various tribes in confrontation against him and tried to extinguish the

Light of Allah. O Allah! You take my revenge from the Quraish because they have ceased to treat me with kindness and they have become accomplice to each other against me. They have deprived me of my right and snatched the government of my brother from me, and have handed over it to such a person who was neither euqal to me with regard to relationship with the Prophet (S.A.W.) nor in precedence to Islam. Besides, the act of presenting of a claim by a pretender is neither in my knowledge nor, in my view, is in the knowledge of Allah. Allah is praiseworthy in all circumstances.

Regarding your charge on Zahhak bin Qais for pillage of the people of Heerah, but the fact is that he is not even able to go near the venue of pillage, what to speak of his own indulgence in it. Yes! he had come with a contingent of horsemen and occupied Samavah and then passed through Waqisa, Sharaf, Qutqutana and the adjacent areas. I deputed a huge army of Muslims. When he heard of it, he felt ashamed, abandoned his operations and fled away fastly. This army chased him and caught him in the way. They (the army) had chased him quite vigorously (so were tired) and the sun was about to set; therefore, they fought for a little while. However, barely an hour had passed, he ran away as he could not face the lightening swords. Among his companions, more than ten were killed, and he being neck entangled and gasping, escaped with great difficulty.

You have asked for my views in the present conditions. In my opinion, we should continue fighting with the apostates till I meet Allah (till my last breath). Neither the multitude of people around me can enhance my honour, nor their separation can bewilder me, because I am truthful and Allah is with the true people. By Allah, I do not abhor at all to die for truth and after death, perfect goodness is for the people on path of truth.

You have offered to come to me with your brothers and

sons, it is not all necessary for me. You stay at your place as a pious guide, worthy of praise, because I do not like that I may die and you may also die along with me. You never consider your brother, whether he is forsaken by all the world and people, a beseecher, an apologiser, kneeling, sufferer of tyranny and oppressiveness for his weakness, a soft girdle or a tame horse for any horseman. He according to the poet of Banu Saleem, is like this:

"If he enquires as how am I (then you hear from me).

I am brave and endurer of misfortunes. It is grievous for me to be seen in ill condition, which may gladden the enemies and sadden the friends." Wassalam.

(Sharh Ibn Abi-al Hadeed vol. 1, p. 155).

(48)

TO ZIYAD IBN KHASAFA ANSARI (R.A.A.)

Abdullah ibn Wal reported that when he was young, Hadrat 'Ali (R.A.A.) sent through him the following letter to Ziyad ibn Khasafah (R.A.A.):

In the Name of Allah, Most Compassionate, Most Merciful

Hereafter:

I had instructed you to stay in Dairabi Musa until you receive my orders. The reason for that was my ignorance about their destination. Now I have come to know that they have gone towards Niffar. Now you locate them. They have murdered a person of learned group during prayers. When you find them, return them to me. If they refuse to do so, fight with them and seek Allah's help in your fight as they have abandoned the truth. They have shed sacred blood and made the path hazardous. Wassalam.

(Tabari, vol. 6, p. 68).

(49)

TO ZIYAD IBN KHASAFA ANSARI (R.A.A.)

Ziyad ibn Khasafah wrote a letter to Hadrat 'Ali (R.A.A.) from Basrah about the incident of Mazar (A place between Wasit and Basrah). The following is the reply given by Hadrat 'Ali (R.A.A.) to his letter:

In the Name of Allah, Most Compassionate, Most Merciful

Hereafter:

I received your letter. I have understood what you have written about Naji and his brothers. Allah has sealed their hearts and Satan has painted in their eyes their misdeeds as virtuous. They roam about conjecturing and think that they are doing good deeds. You have also thrown light on the confrontation which took place between you and them. (Look!) the efforts made by you and your companions are for the sake of Allah and their rewards will also be given by Allah. The smallest reward, from Allah to the people of faith, is far more better than the worldly gains for which people sacrifice themselves, because what you possess (worldly gains) is perishable and what is with Allah (world hereafter) is permanent. (Allah says) He will definitely give recompense to the virtuous deeds of His patient servants. As regards your enemies, with whom you have fought, their forsaking the guidance, falling in vice, rejection of the truth, involvement in mischief and violence, are enough for their ruin. You ignore them and their mischievous doings and let them wander in their insolence. Listen, you will see they will very soon be made captives and killed. You come to me immediately with your companions. Allah will bestow His recompense for this on you and your companions because you have obeyed, carried out orders and well waded - through misery. Wassalam.

(Tabari, vol. 6, p. 70).

(50)

TO HADRAT ABDULLAH IBN ABBAS (R.A.A.)

Hadrat 'Ali (R.A.A.) sent Ma'qil ibn Qais, with two thousand Kufies, to Khirrit and wrote the following letter to the governor of Basrah, Hadrat Abdullah ibn Abbas (R.A.A.):

In the Name of Allah, Most Compassionate, Most Merciful

Hereafter:

Send a dignified brave and reputed pious man with two thousand soldiers following Ma 'qil ibn Qais (to join him). That person will be the commander of the army during his journey from Basrah onwards till he meets Ma'qil. When he meets Ma'qil, the latter will take over the command of both armies, his orders should be carried out, he should be obeyed, and should not be opposed (in any matter); and instruct Ziyad ibn Khasafah to report to me as Ziyad is the best person and his tribe is the best tribe. Wassalam.

(Tabari, vol. 6, p. 70).

(51)

TO MA'QIL IBN QAIS (R.A.A.)

He was a highly brave companion of the Holy Prophet (S.A.W.). On the conquest of Tustar, Hadrat 'Ammar ibn Yaasir (R.A.A.) sent the happy news to Hadrat 'Umar (R.A.A.) by him. He was also commander of army in Battle of Jamal. Hadrat 'Ali (R.A.A.) appointed him as

Police Chief. He was staying with Hadrat Mughirah (R.A.A.) in Kufa when Ibn 'Alqah revolted. Hadrat Mughirah (R.A.A.) sent an army of 3000 soldiers under his command to fight him. A fierce fight took place at the bank of Tigris. Hadrat Ma'qil was martyred there in 43 A.H.

Earlier under the orders of Hadrat Ali (R.A.A.) Ma'qil ibn Qais chased the Khariji rebels and caught them. A heavy fighting took place between them. Three hundred rebels were killed and Khirrit escaped and ran away. When Ma'qil informed Hadrat 'Ali (R.A.A.) about this event, the latter sent the following letter to him:

In the Name of Allah, Most Compassionate, Most Merciful

Hereafter:

For supporting the friends and disgracing the enemies, I offer Praise to Allah. May Allah bestow on you and the Muslims good recompense. You proved yourself up to the mark in trial and you have rendered your worth. (Now) Search for the person of Naji tribe (Khirrit), and when you get information of his presence in a certain city, go there and either kill him or banish him out of country; because he has always been an enemy of Muslims and friend of rejectors of truth, and will also remain so in future. Wassalam.

(Tabari; vol. 6, p. 72).

(52)

TO THE PEOPLE OF KUFA

Haris ibn Ka'ab stated that when Ma'qil ibn Qais came back from the battle, he read to us the following letter of Hadrat 'Ali (R.A.A.):

In the name of Allah, Most Compassionate, Most Merciful

This letter of the servant of Allah, 'Ali, leader of the faithful, is for those before whom it is read, whether they may be Believers, Muslims, Christians or apostates. Allah's peace be on you and on those who followed the truth, and put faith in Allah, the Messenger, the Quran and the resurrection, who fulfilled the promise made with Allah and abstained form breach of trust.

Hereafter:

I invite you to the Book of Allah, Sunnah of the Prophet (S.A.W.) and practice of truth, and for it Allah has ordained them in His Book. Those persons among you who turn back and go to their families, abstain themselves from the fight and separate themselves from that war-mongering man, who is destined to destruction, who has come to fight with Allah, His Messenger and Muslims, and excites disturbance on earth, shall have guarantee of protection of their lives and property. And for those who will follow them in fight against us and disobey us, we will pray for Allah's help against them and bring Allah in between and He is enough for the help. Wassalam.
(Tabari, vol. 6, p. 73).

(53)

TO HIS COMPANIONS

When the battle of Nahravan ended, Hujr ibn 'Abi' Amar ibn al-Hamiq and 'Abdullah ibn Wahb al Rasi (R.A.A.) came to Hadrat 'Ali (R.A.A.) and enquired of his opinion about Hadrat Abu Bakr, Hadrat Umar and Hadrat Usman (R.A.A.). Hadrat 'Ali said "(Are you concerned at this time about these matters?); Are you absolved of the existing problems? Enemy has occupied Egypt, my companions and supporters have been martyred; (But you are occupied with these matters. However, to satisfy you), I will give you a detailed statement in which I will explain all about those queries which you have made. You may read that statement to my companions." Thereupon he wrote the following statement:

In the Name of Allah, Most Compassionate, Most Merciful

Hereafter:

Allah sent Hadrat Muhammad (S.A.W.), as warner to the whole world, trustee of His Book and witness to this Ummah. O people of Arabia! You were unbelievers, lived in miserable condition, shed blood of each other among yourselves, killed your children, cut off the ties of kinship, and unjustly appropriated the property of each other. Allah, conferring His favour on you, sent His Messenger Hadrat Muhammad (S.A.W.) who spoke your language towards you and in consequence, you accepted the faith. Hadrat Muhammad (S.A.W.) belonged to you and lived among you. You are well aware of him and his geneology. He taught you the Book of Allah, Wisdom, his Sunnah and your duties. He instructed you to offer kind treatment to your relatives, abstain from blood-shedding, improve your conditions, return things given in one's trust to their owners, honour the promise, and enjoined you to treat all kindly, help and be compassionate to each other, and prohibited you from cruelty, jealousy, abusing, defiance, liquor-drinking, short measuring and weighing and presented to you the command of Allah to abstain from fornication and also not to usurp the property of orphans. He (the Prophet S.A.W.) persuaded you to emulate all those virtues which keep you away from the Hell and prohibited you from all those evils which take you away from Paradise. When his (Holy Prophet's) time-limit of existence in the world came to an end, Allah called him back from this world in spite of his laudable endeavours, pleasing deeds, remission of all his slips and holding a high status before Allah. Alas! from his passing away the Muslims in general, and his relatives in particular, had to bear great adversity.

When the Prophet (S.A.W.) departed from this mortal world, disputes arose among Muslims about Caliphate and authority. By Allah! it did not occur to my mind and imagination that Arabs would shift it (the caliphate) from me (to any other party). As such, I was astonished on people's response and rush towards Abu Bakr (R.A.A.). I withheld my hand (from offering allegiance) (because) I noted that among all people I was the most rightful successor of Hadrat Muhammad (S.A.W.) than the person posted caliph over me. Consequently, I remained firm on that stand as long as Allah so desired (I did not offer the allegiance). But when I felt that many people had retracted from the faith and busily indulged in the attempt of destroying the religion of Muhammad (S.A.W.) and Ibrahim, I was afraid, if I did not come to rescue of Islam and Muslims, the religion would be exposed to disintegration and damage, and that disastrous situation would be much more (painful) than my deprival from the caliphate which resembled to a short-term wealth destined to vanish one day like a mirage. Therefore, I stood up and took oath of allegiance on the hand of Abu Bakr (R.A.A.) and began to work side by side with him to meet the situations until the falsehood was demolished and in spite of opposition from infidels the "Kalima" of Allah soared high. Abu Bakr (R.A.A.), after assuming the caliphate, treated people mildly, led them on straight path, saved (them) from exaggeration and exercised moderation. In these affairs, I remained with him as a well-wishing companion and followed him in all his efforts made in service to Allah.

When death approached Abu Bakr (R.A.A.), he handed over the caliphate to Umar (R.A.A.). I accepted his decision, obeyed Umar (R.A.A.), took oath of allegiance on his hand and served as a good adviser to him. On becoming the trustee of (state) affairs, Umar remained throughout a person of good nature and a caliph of honourable character and of chaste spirit.

When the time of his death came near, I thought in my mind that now the caliphate would not shift from me. But Umar set up an advisory committee, in which I was also placed a sixth member. For the members of that advisory committee, assumption of Caliphate by me was most unpleasing than the government of any one else, because they were aware of my altercations and argumentaion with Abu Bakr (R.A.A.) and I sued to say "O people of Quraish, I am the most rightful of caliphate among you until there exists a single reciter of the Quran and familiar with Sunnah (till doomsday)". All this made them afraid that if I took over as caliph, they wold not have any share in the caliphate. Therefore, they unanimously decided to offer allegiance to any one excepting me. Thus, they withdrawing caliphate from me, assigned it to Usman and excluded me in the hope that whenever they would be disappointed in securing the power, they would (in the same way) transfer it among themselves. Then, they asked me to offer allegiance to Usman, otherwise they would fight with me. Consequently, I had to offer allegiance unwillingly and I kept patience for the sake of Allah. One of them even charged me that "O son of Abu Talib, you are very covetous of caliphate." I retorted that he was more covetous than me. I was only demanding the heritage of my brother and my right for it; and you, without any reason, stood as an obstacle between me and the heritage and were dragging me away from that. O Allah! I seek Thy help against Quraish. Look! they have severed the relations, reduced my high position and superiority and united to snatch my right which I deserve much more than them. Then, they said to me, "Now you grieve for it and lament for the rest of your life. I looked around myself but did not find any friend or sympathiser except the members of the family. I did not like to get my family members to be killed. Therefore, I turned away my eyes from the rubbish and endured the grief, and by controlling my indignation, I put up with such a distress which was more bitter than wild bitter fruit and more agonising to heart than the red hot iron. Then you put blames on Usman, stormed on him and assassinated him.

Thereafter, you came to offer allegiance to me. Neither I nor you reached to an agreement. On this you began to argue with me. But to save myself from you, I did not stretch my hand (for taking oath of allegiance). Then you fell upon me in a way that I felt as if you would kill each other or even me; thereafter you stated that you did not find anyone (competent) except me and would not be unanimous on anyone else except me, therefore you requested me to accept your allegiance and/ from now on there would not be any difference or division between us. On this (assurance) I took oath of allegiance from you. You also invited others to follow suit. As such one who, with free will and pleasure, offered his allegiance to me, I accepted it and the others who refused, I left them to their state. Thus, first of all who offered their allegiance to me were Talha and Zubair (R.A.A.). Had they refused allegiance to me I would have not compelled them as in case of others. They stood firm on it for a few days, when I received the news that both of them have departed to Basrah with an army in which every individual had offered allegiance to me or assented his obedience to me. They attacked my administrators in Basrah, on the godowns and offices of my public treasuries and the people of the city, who were all obedient to me and also my friends, and disintegrated their society, and maligned the party supporting me. They, they ran over my companions, killed some of them fradulently, slew some in prisons and put others on sword till those innocents patiently met Allah in hope of recompense. By Allah! if they had killed even a single man intentionally, it would have been lawful for me to kill their entire army, whereas they martyred so may Muslims who exceeded them in number. May Allah help us against them and destroy the tyrants.

Then I looked towards the people of Syria and found

them highly stupid, greedy, foolish and mean, who had collected from here and there. They were worthy of being educated and disciplined, guarded and checked by employing an officer over them. Neither they belonged to emigrants nor Ansar, nor the noble successors of the companions of the Prophet (S.A.W.). I had to fight with them. First I invited them to unity and obedience, which they rejected and remained steadfast to disunity and division and arraying themselves against the emigrants, Ansar and noble successors of the companions of the Prophet (S.A.W.) started wounding them by their arrows and spears. Thereupon I also hurriedly advanced for the combat and started fighting with them. When our weapons commenced slaying and inflicted painful wounds, they raised high the Quran and invited you towards the injunctions of Quran. On this, I warned you to realise that they were neither pious nor followers of Quran; they raised high the Quran only to deceive you; urged you to carry on fighting with them. But you accused me and advised me to accept their offer because if they obeyed the injunction of Quran then they would join us on the truth which we were following and if they did not do so then this act would be final argument for us against them. On this I had to accept their offer and withdrew my hands from fighting. It was decided that two persons be appointed as arbitrators, who should maintain those things which the Quran maintains and abolish those which the Quran abolished. But difference of opinion arose among the two arbitrators and they delivered two separate decisions by ignoring the injunctions of Quran, acted against Quran and followed their own wishes against the guidance of Allah. Allah also digressed them from the right path and led them on wrong path which they deserve. Then, one of their group deserted us. Consequently, so long they remained aloof,we also remained unconcerned. But when they started mischiefs and creating distrubance, and martyred Muslims, we called upon them and demanded to hand over the assassinators of our brothers. They said that they all jointly had killed them and they all consider lawful killing them as well as me. (After saying this) their cavalries and platoons launched a violent attack on us and Allah also defeated them like other tyrants. Then I ordered you to chase the enemies without pausing, as that would frighten them, their imposture would come to an end and fraud revealed. On this you said, "Our wrists are tired, our swords have become blunt, our arrow stock has finished,and the heads of our spears have become loose. Now you allow us to go back, make extensive preparations, and when we return, we may have added as many persons among fighters as our people have been martyred or died; because against enemies, this is our strength." Thereafter when you came back and encamped at Kufa, I commanded you to stay in cantonment area, associate those who deflected and be prepared for war, and avoid frequent visits to your families as that would generate affection in your hearts and (this act) would make you tender and lenient. (Listen!) until a fighter takes the revenge and attains his object (victory), he does not mourn for anyone,nor get quarulous for anything, neither wakefulness of night nor thirst of day and pang of hunger pester them. On this (observation) some of you left for the city after offering their apology and others by violating the orders. Then, one had joined me under compulsion, did not stick to his decision and he who went to city did not return. When I looked upon my army only 50 of you were present. Finding this position I also came to you (in the city). Then, up to this day you have not been able to set out with me for fight. May Allah guide you to practise virtue! What makes you to wait for? Do you not see that your territories are deminishing? Egypt has gone out of your control. Why have you lost your senses! Look! the opponents have already united and they have started making preparations. They possess fellow feeling for each other and you are still indulging in disunity, discord and dissension. (Look) Even now if you unite, you will succeed. May Allah's blessing be on you! Awake those who are still in sleep among you and be prepared to combat the enemy. (Do you know with whom you have to fight?). Your fight is with Tulaqa (People granted amnesty at the time of conquest of Makkah) and their descendants who accepted Islam perforce and continued their fight throughout with the Prophet (S.A.W.), who are enemy of (both) Quran and Sunnah, participants of Battle of Ahzab, introducers of innovation, whose residual deeds are to be abstained, are apostates of faith; acceptors of bribe and servants of worldly temptation. I have got the news that the son of notorious mother (Amar ibn Al-Aas) did not offer his allegiance to Mu'awiya until he settled his term receiving such a heavy bribe, which surpasses the value of his entire state (Egypt). May Allah empty the hands of that who has sold his faith for the worldly wealth, and destroy the hands of the purchaser of the support of a treacherous sinner by public money. They included also those people who have drunk liquor[1] in your gatherings and underwent punishment of whipping according to Islamic law, and the same people (today) have assumed the leadership of the nation. The one, among them whose vices I have not mentioned, is excessively wicked and pernicious. They are the people, who, if become your rulers, they will retaliate with you, feel proud, rule with cruelty, practise violence in anger, and spread mischief and disturbance in the country. Furthermore, they will follow their lust and never make correct decisions.

You are, in spite of your disunity and non-practicality, much better and righteous than those people. Among you are philosophers, religious scholars, theologians, memorizers of Quran, offerers of midnight prayers, worshippers, recluses, offerers of prayers and reciters of Quran. Will you not feel grievous and unpleasant that these idiots,mean and

---

1. It hints to Walid ibn 'Utbah, who was step brother of Hadrat Usman (R.A.A.) and governor of Kufa in 23 A.H. during the caliphate of Usman (R.A.A.). He was found guilty of drinking and was awarded the punishment by the Caliph, Hadrat Usman (R.A.A.) and was dismissed from the governorship.

mischievous people are trying to snatch government from you?

(Look!) When I say anything, listen it and when I give you an order, obey it and when I render advice to you, understand it and rely on my policy, when I firmly decide a thing, you follow it; you rise when I rise and fight with him with whom I fight.

(Remember!) In disobeying me, you will not get the guidance and fail to unite. Therefore, you take up your arms for war,make preparation for it because the fire of war has flared up and its flames have soared high, and tyrants are trying tooth and nail to extinguish the light of Allah and overpower you and make you a target of their wrath.

O servants of Allah! Look, the destruction of the companions of satan, greedies and tyrants and their exertion in perverseness and following of falsehood can never be superior than the endeavours of the pious, honest, true and faithful people in obedience to Allah and support to the leader. By Allah! if I fight with them alone, whereas the whole world supports them, even then I shall not care and won't be embarrassed by them. In the affair of their perverseness and my righteousness, I believe on my insight and have reasons and arguments for it. And I do long for meeting with my Lord, and am expectant and desirous for his best recompense. But my heart grieves and laments on this that the foolish and vicious ruler of this Ummah transfer the wealth of Allah from hand to hand, make captive the servants of Allah, fight the virtuous and join with the vicious. By Allah! if this situation had not prevailed, I would not have made my best efforts to unite, collect and stir you up but would have left you (in your position) to your fate.

By Allah! I am on right and love martyrdom. (Look!) If Allah wished so, I shall move, along with you, for war. Go forth light armed and heavy armed and strive with you wealth and with your lives in the way of Allah. Certainly Allah is with the patients.

(9:41) (*Al Imamat wal Syasat, vol.1, p.113*).

(54)

TO HADRAT MASQALAH BIN HUBAIRAH

Hadrat Ali (R.A.A.) wrote the following letter to Hadrat Masqalah and sent to him by Abu Jurrah Hanafi:

In the Name of Allah, Most Compassionate, Most Merciful

Hereafter: Breach of trust with Ummah is the highest kind of treachery, and cheating the leader is the most grievous cheating with the people of the city. You immediately return the 5 lakh Dirham,[1] which you have in your possession which is the right of Muslims, as soon as my messenger reaches you, otherwise you report to me at once on receipt of this order. I have already instructed my messenger not to allow you respite for a moment for the despatch of the amount after he reaches you. Wassalam.

(Tabari, vol. 6, p. 75).

(55)

TO THE SHIAS OF KUFA

It is reported that when Hadrat Ali (R.A.A.) encamped for a few days at Nukhailah, people began to slip away to Kufa and only a contingent of about a thousand people remained with him. When he noticed this position he also went to Kufa and stayed there. When he noted that the people of Kufa hesitated to fight along with him against people of Syria and he got the news that the cavalry of Hadrat Mu'awiya

1. Hadrat Masqalah freed a few Muslim captives, after a deal of purchase but did not deposit the price. On demand for payment, he ran away to Hadrat Mu'awiya (R.A.A.) and became his ally.

(R.A.A.), after reaching Anbar,[1] slayed his one platoon and plundered Anbar, he wrote the following letter and sent through a person, directing him to read it before the congregation after the completion of Juma prayers.

In the Name of Allah, Most Compassionate, Most Merciful

This letter is from the servant of Allah, 'Ali, the leader of faithful, to his party of Kufa. May Allah's peace be on you!

Hereafter:

War in the way of Allah is one of the entrances of Paradise. One who forsakes it, Allah clothes him with the dress of disgrace and covers him with the sheet of contempt in such a way that the stamp of wretchedness is affixed on him and he is subjected to the tyranny and oppression of others. (Look!) I invited you day in and night, openly and secretly (in every way) for religious war and advised you to attack them before their onslaught, because the people in whose territory war is fought, are disgraced and demoralized and their enemy becomes bold over them. A man from the tribe of Bani 'Aamir came to Anbar and killed ibn Hassan Bikri, repulsed your armed soldiers, martyred many pious persons, and I got the news, that they entered the homes of Muslim and convented women, took off anklets from their feet and necklaces from their necks and then returned with complete success. Not a single person of them received even a scratch, If any one dies lamenting on it, in my view, is not subject to reproach at all, because this (incident) deserves that. How astonishing is the attitude which weakens the hearts, enhances sorrow and increases grief, that people unite on falsehood and you continue divided on truth. Allah may destroy you and keep you away from His Blessing ! You have become the target, arrows after arrows are being shot at you, but you do not shoot

2. A place in Iran on the eastern bank of Euphrates, were the army of Islam, under the command of Hadrat Khalid (R.A.A.), had landed.

arrows. Raids after raids are being made on you but you do not raid. Disobedience to Allah is rampant and you are contented with it. When I ask you in the winter season to move for war, you say, "How can we fight in this severe cold?" And when I ask you in summer, you say, "Let the severity of heat lessen." All these things indicate your liking for escape from death. When you seek protection from cold and heat in this way, you will, by Allah, run away more speedily away from the sword. I swear by that Supreme authority in Whose control is my soul, that your fight is not from these (heat and cold) but you seek safety from sword. O males, nay male-like persons! O confused dreams of children; O bearers of feminine mentality reared in ornamented chambers, I, by Allah, like that Allah may separate me from you and bring me under His blessing (I prefer death than to live among You). Had I not seen you or associated with you! By Allah, you have saturated my heart from indignation, engulfed me in great bitterness and by your disobedience and abandoning submission to me, you have made fallible my judgement to such an extent that the Quraish are remarking, "Although the son of Abu Talib is brave but is not aware of the strategy of war." How surprising is this! Is there anyone among them who possesses more experience, expertise of war, than me? I have entered the field of war at the age of less than 20 years and now I am above sixty years of age. This is not the point, the point is that the judgement of that person has no weight who is not followed and obeyed. Wassalam.

(Al-Akhbar-al-Tiwal p. 225)

(56)

TO ABUL ASWAD (R.A.A.)

Hadrat Abul Aswad was one of the highly educated and intelligent successors of the companions of Holy Prophet (S.A.W.). According to Allama Zahbi, he was a judge of Basrah during the Caliphate of Hadrat 'Ali

(R.A.A.). He was the first expert in clarifying the syntax of grammar. He participated in the battle of Siffin. He died in 99 A.H. from paralysis.

Abul Asward wrote to the caliph that your cousin, Abdullah Ibn 'Abbas (R.A.A.) has devoured the wealth in his possession without your knowledge and information. I cannot hide this fact from you. Therefore, consider Allah's kindness to you in this. The leader of the faithful replied to him, as under :

In the Name of Allah, Most Compassionate, Most Merciful

Hereafter:

People like you, are wellwisher of the leader and Ummah (both, of ruler and public), return the things, keep the trust and guide to the truth. I have written to your friend about the issue which you have informed me without giving the indication that you have written me about it. Therefore, you keep me informed of all such matters which come to your notice, as keeping watch on them lies the welfare and prosperity of Ummah, because you are competent to do so and fulfilment of this right (of Ummah) is obligatory on you. Wassalam. *(Tabari, vol. 6, p. 82).*

(57)

TO ABDULLAH IBN ABBAS (R.A.A.)

Hadrat 'ali (R.A.A.) wrote the following letter to Hadrat Abdullah Ibn Abbas (R.A.A.):

In the Name of Allah, Most Compassionate, Most Merciful

I associated you in my trust (government), made you partner and took you in confidence because in my view there was none in my family more reliable than you. But when you saw that the time was oppressing you cousin and enemy was at war with him, you withdrew your support to him and forsook him like others, and did not help him like others. You grabbed the wealth of Ummah, on which you could get hold of like a speedy wolf which drags away a wounded she-goat. Look! You pause (and think over) of the time when you have completed your life and your actions are being presented at that place where the arrogant person cries stricken in grief and the violator of rights yearns for penitence, and tyrant for return again to the world (for making good the loss), although the road for escape has been closed (then what you will do at that time). Wassalam.

(Nahj-ul-Balaghah, p. 767).

(58)

TO HADRAT ABDULLAH IBN ABBAS (R.A.A.)

Hadrat 'Ali (R.A.A.) wrote the following letter to Hadrat Abdullah ibn Abbas (R.A.A.)

In the Name of Allah, Most Compassionate, Most Merciful

I have been informed about an allegation against you. If it is correct (that you have taken in your personal use some portion of public treasury) then you have annoyed your Lord, disobeyed your leader, idsgraced your trustworthiness and committed breach of trust of the Muslims.

I have also learnt that you have laid waste the land, and have seized that which was under your possession and consumed that which has been in you hand. Therefore, you send your account and fully understand that the reckoning of Allah is more severe than the reckoning of people. Wassalam.

(Al Iqd-ul-Farid, vol. 2, p. 242).

(59)

FROM AND TO HADRAT ABDULLAH IBN ABBAS (R.A.A)

When Hadrat Abdullah Ibn Abbas (R.A.A.) received the above noted letter of Hadrat 'Ali (R.A.A.), he wrote the following reply to the leader of the faithful:

In the Name of Allah, Most Compassionate, Most Merciful

After praise and eulogy of Allah, (I beg to say) that the information you have received is entirely incorrect. The wealth in my control is intact and I am guarding it. You please do not take these misgivings (of people) as correct. Wassalam.

In reply, Hadrat 'Ali (R.A.A.) wrote:

In the Name of Allah, Most Compassionate, Most Merciful

Hereafter:

Inform me what you have collected as tribute, from where received and how you have spent it? Wassalam.

(Tabari, vol. 6, p. 82).

(60)

TO HADRAT ABDULLAH IBN ABBAS (R.A.A.)

When Hadrat Abdullah ibn Abbas received the letter of Hadrat 'Ali (R.A.A.), he replied that his share was much more in public treasury than that which he has taken from it. In reply, Hadrat 'Ali wrote the following letter to him:

In the Name of Allah, Most Compassionate, Most Merciful

Hereafter:

This deception of yourself to you is highly surprising that you have obtained less than your right from the public treasury. You are like an ordinary Muslim. You know well the formerly great people of Badr, who never took more than their fixed share. For your chastisement (in Hereafter) it is enough that you have settled in Makkah, and while residing there, you purchase the articles of Madinah and Taif, whatever you see and like, notwithstanding the fact that in this (purchase) the wealth of others is spent.

By Allah! I never like that the wealth of Muslims which I rightfully obtain, I should leave it after me as my inheritance. (You presume) as if you have died and tomorrow your actions will be presented before you on resurrection, when the destroyer of virtue prays for penitence and absolution but cannot obtain salvation. Wassalam.

(Al-Iqdul-Farid, vol. 2, p. 243).

(61)

TO HADRAT ABDULLAH IBN ABBAS (R.A.A.)

It is reported that Hadrat 'Ali (R.A.A.) wrote the following letter also to Hadrat Abdullah ibn Abbas:

In the Name of Allah, Most Compassionate, Most Merciful

Lo! A clear proof has come unto you from your Lord, so give full measure and full weight and do not give short to people and do not create disturbance on the earth after its reformation; if you are a believer, it will be better for you. (7:85)

As you read this letter, immediately preserve safely the wealth of your government which is in your possession, unlit my receiver comes to you. Wassalam.

(Kifayat-ul-Matalib, p. 147)

(62)

TO HADRAT ABDULLAH IBN ABBAS (R.A.A)

Hadrat 'Ali wrote the following letter to Hadrat Abdullah ibn Abbas (R.A.A.)

In the Name of Allah, Most Compassionate, Most Merciful

The acquisition of a thing sometimes pleases a man, which he deems in his permanent possession and sometimes the deprival of a thing leaves him sad, which is not destined for him. Therefore, neither feel too happy on getting a worldly thing nor bevail on deprival of anything. Your happiness should be only for earning something for the Hereafter, and lamentation be only for loosing something in Hereafter, and your concern should only be for that which will follow after death.

(Aijaz-ul-Quran, p. 121).

(63)

TO HADRAT MU'AWIYA (R.A.A.)

Hadrat 'Ali (R.A.A.) sent the following letter in reply to the letter of Hadrat Mu'awiya (R.A.A.):

In the Name of Allah, Most Compassionate, Most Merciful

I received your letter in which you have mentioned about the selection of (Hadrat) Muhammad (S.A.W.) by Allah for His religion and providing him the strength from those companions who supported him. Is it so that the time had kept you informed of may wonderful secrets which were hidden form me? You are giving me the information about the beneficence and reward of Allah granted to us! (In other words) you are being the carrier of dates to Hajar (a great centre of dates) (i.e. like carrier of coal to New Castle) or throwing a challenge to your instructor for archery (trying to instruct one already well-versed in archery). In your view, certain (selected) persons hold superiority in Islam. You have stated such a thing which if becomes true, you will remain excluded from them, and if it is not so, the loss suffered from that will not elevate you (in no way you will receive any gain). Well! How you know who is superior and who is inferior? Who is administrator and who is to be administered? Well! What right Tulaqa (the people freed on amnesty after conquest of Makkah) and their descendants have to create distinction between the first line of emigrants , determine their ranks and establish categories in them? Alas! such a whizzing sound emanated from the shooting arrow which is not found in other arrows (you are apprising your pride on the superiority of others) and the subordinates have started issuing orders (to superiors). O man! will you not stick to your position; or assess your low strength and not stay where your fate has dragged you in? Neither the defeat of any over powered is your defeat, nor the victory of any conqueror is your conquest. You are running fast towards straying and have been misled from the right path.

Look! Not for conveying news to you, I am recounting to you bounties of Allah (on us). The emigrants and Ansar who were martyred in the way of Allah, were all superior persons. (But) one martyr from us was such who was given the title of Syedush-shuhda (leader of martyrs) and the Prophet (S.A.W.), in his funeral prayer, offered seventy Takbirs (Allah-o-Akbar) and thus gave him (Hadrat Hamza (R.A.A.)) a singularity. Are you not aware that all those whose arm were amputated in the way of Allah, rank superior. (But) one of us was given the honour which none else got. He was given the title of Zul-Janahain (having two wings) and the 'Bird of Paradise' meaning (Hadrat Ja'far Tayyar R.A.A.). If Allah had not prohibited (His servants) from self-praising, I, the describer, would have enumerated many virtues (of my own self) (and these would have been the same) which the faithful already know and those would not have burdened the ears of listeners.

Therefore, you forsake the servants of the world (who are misleading you and inciting you for caliphate) because we are special creatures of Allah and people have been later created for us.

Our ancient honour and old superiority vis-a-vis your people did not prevent us from associating you with us.

Therefore, we married your daughters and gave our daughters in marriage to you as if you were equal to us in rank and status, whereas you were not worthy of that. And how you could be equal to us when the Prophet (S.A.W.) was from us and the belier of Prophethood (Abu Sufyan R.A.A.) was from you, the Lion of Allah (Asad-Allah) (Hadrat 'Ali himself) was from us and lion of Ahlaf[1] ('Utba ibn Rabi'a) from you; two leaders of the youths of Paradise from us (Hadrat Hasan and Hadrat Husain) and youths of Hell[2] (captives of Badr) from you; and the best of all women of the time (Hadrat Fatima R.A.A.) from us and collector of thorns and fuel wood[3] (Umm-i-Jameel, wife of Abu Lahab) from you. Besides, we have been bestowed many virtues vis-a-vis you.

Our Islam is also known the world over and our ignorance has also been unassailable. Then whatever

---

1. In the Battle of Badr, Utba ibn Rabi'a the famous warrior of the infidels of Makkah came in the war field and challenged for fight. Hadrat 'Ali came to fight him. He asked "who are you?" Hadrat Ali replied, "Asad-Allah, the Lion of Allah". Utba said, "I am also Asad-ul-Alhaf" i.e. the lion of that group which pledged to oppress the Prophet (S.A.W.).
2. "Hellish youth" original 'Sabit-un-Nar. It refers to 'Aqaba ibn Abi Moeet, who oppressed the Prophet (S.A.W.) very much. In the battle of Badr, he was taken as captive. Holy Prophet (S.A.W.) got him killed and said the fire of Hell is for him.
3. This is Umme Jameel bint Harb, w/o Abu Lahab who used to bring thorns from jungle and spread along the way of the Prophet (S.A.W.).

deficiency remained in us, was replenished by Quran and that was following Allah's mandate:

"And those who are akin are nearer one to another in the ordinance of Allah." (8:75) This is also Allah's command. "Lo! those of mankind who have the best claim to Abraham are those who followed him, and this Prophet and those who believe (with him); and Allah is the Protecting Friend of the believers." (3:68)

Now we are also superior and venerable according to the kinship as well as obedience. The emigrants presented to Ansar the argument of nearness with the Prophet (S.A.W.) and they were successful (it was decided that caliphate will go the Emigrants). In consequence, when success was achieved on this basis, we are truly rightful claimant vis-a-vis you and if success had not been achieved, Ansar's claim still remains there.

According to your view, I have envied all the caliphs and revolted against all of them. If it is a fact, even then this is not a crime (against you) for which I should offer my apology to you. You are putting that blame on me in which (I am) not involved about.

You have written that I was dragged like a nose-stringed camel for taking oath of allegiance. In this allegation, by Allah, you intended to condemn us but (mistakenly) happened to praise me; you tried to disgrace us but you yourself have been disgraced. Muslim, subjected to oppression is not to be blamed unless he is shaken in his faith and belief. I have quoted this argument about caliphate (not for you) against others, and all that had occurred I have not described you in its entirety.

Then, you have mentioned about the affairs between me and 'Usman (R.A.A.). You have a right for my answer in that respect because you are relative of 'Usman (R.A.A.) (Lo! you yourself tell me) who was the stark enemy of 'Usman (R.A.A.) between me and you, who created the causes of his assassination? Either he who extended his help was not accepted, or he from whom he requested for help but he (you) drew back and pushed death towards him, until his assassination took place. Look! by Allah, Allah knows very well those among you withheld their help, and those who invited people to secure their shelter and those who saved their skin from the involvement in fight.

Yes! I have not to present any apology for the fact that I objected to the innovation of 'Usman (R.A.A.) However, if even my offer of guidance or reformation is my fault, then many innocent people have been facing condemnation and many counsellors have been subjected to accusations.

I desire naught save reform so far as I am able. My welfare is only in Allah. In Him I trust and unto Him I turn (repentant). *(11:88)*

You have written that you have only sword for me and my companions; thus you have caused us to laugh from mourning. (We mourned on this issue that you were demanding that thing from me for which you had no right; now I burst into laugh at your offer). When did you find the descendants of Abdul Muttalib hesitant to fight the enemies and afraid of their swords? Wait a little! the confrontation is about to take place. Very soon he will challenge you whom are challenging (today) and that thing (war) will be close to you from which you are trying to keep away.

I am going to advance forward towards you very soon, with an army comprising of excellent emigrants, Ansar (residents of Madinah) and the best followers of the companions of the Prophet (S.A.W.), which is very huge in number and whose cloud of dust in trail will be too wide. They have put on the shroud as their dress and are too keen to meet their Lord. They are supported by the brave fighters of Badr and armed with Hashmi swords, from the sharp cutting of which your own brother, maternal uncle, maternal grand father and (about) your family (at Badr) already have experienced and these are not far away from the tyrants.

(*Nahj-al-Balaghah, vol. 2, p.21*)

(64)

TO KA'B IBN MAALIK (R.A.A.)

Ka'b ibn Maalik (R.A..A.) ibn Ka'b al-Qain was a learned person among Ansar. His father accepted Islam on the occasion of Bai'at-i-Aqaba.

Hadrat 'Ali (R.A.A.) wrote the following letter to his governor Ka'b ibn Maalik (R.A.A):

In the Name of Allah, Most Compassionate, Most Merciful

Hereafter:

You appoint someone else to officiate you and depart with a contingent of your companions for the territory of Sawad[1] and visit each and every village collecting information from the ibhabitants about their governors and testing their character, reach the people inhabited in the and between Tigris and Euphrates. From their turn back to Beh-qabazat[2] and shoulder the responsibility of extending help to them; and manage your government by obeying Allah and understand it well that the world is to perish and the Hereafter is to come. And each deed of every man remains secure for him; and you will definitely get punishment for your misdeeds and whatever good deeds you have performed, you will get its reward. Therefore, perform good deeds to gain good reward. Wassalam.

(Kitab-al-Kharaj, p. 141).

---

1. Territory of Iraq called Sawad for its greenery and fertility.
2. Three villages on the bank of Euphrates.

BIOGRAPHY OF HADRAT 'ALI (R.A.A)

Genealogy and family

Hadrat Ali (R.A.A.) bin Abi Talib Bin Abdul Muttalib bin Hashim bin 'Abd Manaf bin Qusai bin Klaab bin Murrah bin K'ab bin Luvai bin Ghalib bin Fah'r. Fah'r was known by the title of Quraish and therefore the Quraish tribe started from him. Ten tribes emanated from Quraish on the names of its Ten talented, distinguished persons, and Hashim was one of them. Holy Prophet (S.A.W.) and Hadrat 'Ali (R.A.A.) are his descendants. Hashim was entrusted the service of pilgrims. His duty was to provide meals and drinking water and their other necessary comforts. When he died, his wife was pregnant. After a few days a son was born and he was named Shebah. The posthumous son of Hashim, Shebah, was brought up by his brother Muttalib and therefore was famous by the name of Abdul Muttalib, i.e. fostered by Muttalib.

Abdul Muttalib had ten sons, famous among them were Abu Lahab, Abu Talib, Abdullah, Hamzah and Abbas. Hadrat 'Ali was the son of Abu Talib, born from his cousin wife, Fatimah bin Asad bin Hashim. Abu Talib was counted among knowned person and was a well known orator of his time.

Birth, Name

According to famous report, Hadrat 'Ali (R.A.A.) was born in Makkah on 13th Rajab 600 (A.D.) Holy Prophet (S.A.W.) gave first bath by his own hands, put Saliva in his mouth and named him 'Ali, although the name Haider was given earlier by his mother. Because of large family and limited income of Abu Talib, father of Hadrat 'Ali (R.A.A.), and real uncle of the Prophet (S.A.W.), the Holy Prophet (S.A.W.) himself took him under his care and himself bore the financial burden.

Education and Training

The facts about his childhood are obscure but observing

his subsequent life, scholastic abilities, knowledge of language and expertise in military skill, every man had to accept that his education and training was carried out under special supervision, and definitely done so, because his guardian was a person like Hadrat Muhammad (S.A.W.) who was himself the greatest Educator, reformer, and every effort would have been made in that respect.

Titles and Surnames

Hadrat 'Ali had many titles, of which Ghalib and Asadullah were famous. His surnames were Abul Hasan, Abul Husain, Abu Muhammad, Abu Turab, etc.

Acceptance of Islam

At the time when Holy Prophet Muhammad (S.A.W.) was commissioned to Prophethood, he was 10 years old. When the Holy Prophet (S.A.W.) proclaimed the message of Islam, the first to accept the message was a woman, Hadrat Khadija (R.A.A.) wife of the Prophet (S.A.W.), a child, Hadrat 'Ali (R.A.A.), a free man, Hadrat Abu Bakr (R.A.A.) and a slave, Hadrat Zaid bin Harisah. Hadrat 'Ali (R.A.A.) himself mentioned that Hadrat Muhammad (S.A.W.) was appointed as Prophet on Monday and he accepted Islam on Tuesday and also he and Hadrat Ja'far (R.A.A.) had the honour of offering prayers with the Holy Prophet (S.A.W.) in the mountains of Makkah.

Migration of the Holy Prophet (S.A.W.)

The ever-increasing flow of the people in the fold of Islam made the Quraish of Makkah to oppose Islam formally and in a well organised way and they started to oppress the Muslims. By that time, some important persons of Makkah had embraced Islam. As the situation hardened the Prophet (S.A.W.) to save the companions from the unbearable atrocities of the infidels of Makkah permitted to migrate to Madinah and many companions actually left Makkah for Madinah. Later, in 13th year of Prophethood, the Holy Prophet (S.A.W.) was also commanded by Allah to migrate. He (S.A.W.) directed Hadrat Ali (R.A.A.) to sleep on his bed in the night covering himself with a sheet, as he would depart for Madinah on the same night. He (S.A.W.) further directed Hadrat 'Ali (R.A.A.) to return the things kept in his (Prophet's) trust, to their owners and then himself departed for Madinah. That night was a very dangerous night because the infidels had made a plan to kill the Holy Prophet (S.A.W.) on that night and Hadrat 'Ali (R.A.A.) willingly and without any hesitation accepted the order of the Prophet (S.A.W.). When the infidels entered that night into the house of the Prophet (S.A.W.) with their bare swords, they were astonished to find Hadrat 'Ali (R.A.A.) in the bed. After interrogation, they left Hadrat 'Ali (R.A.A.), who in the morning, returned the things kept in Holy Prophet's trust, to their owners, and departed for Madinah on foot.

Brotherhood between Muhajireen and Ansar

After arriving at Madinah, the Prophet (S.A.W.) established brotherhood between Muhajireen (emigrants) and Ansar (Helpers — Muslim residents of Madinah). All the people collected in the house of Anas bin Malik (R.A.A.). The number of emigrants was 34. He called Ansar and told them that the emigrants were your brothers and then severally combined an emigrant with an Ansari and made them brothers. On the turn of Hadrat 'Ali, the Prophet (S.A.W.) said that we both are brothers.

Marriage with Hadrat Fatima (R.A.A.)

After the end of the Battle of Suwaiq in 2 A.H. when the Prophet (S.A.W.) relaxed to some extent, received requests for the marriage with Hadrat Fatima (R.A.A.) began to pour in, Consequently, he married Hadrat Fatimah (R.A.A.) with Hadrat 'Ali (R.A.A.), in the same year. Hadrat 'Ali, who was so long living with the Prophet (S.A.W.) shifted to the house of Harisah bin Nouman (R.A.A.). Holy Prophet (S.A.W.) also provided Hadrat 'Ali (R.A.A.) household articles as he had none. These were one cot, one leather bed filled with the leaves of date, one leather bottle for water, a small water skin, two grind stones, and two earthen water-pots.

The Battles fought in company of the Holy Prophet (S.A.W.)

Hadrat 'Ali (R.A.A.) was generally appointed as the standard-bearer of the battles fought by the Prophet (S.A.W.). Hadrat 'Ali (R.A.A.) performed signal services in the battles and proved himself worthy of the high post. He killed 21 enemies in Battle of Badr, and 22 in Battle of Uhud. In Battle of Trenches, he killed the famous horseman of the infidels Amr bin abdwud, and demoralised the army of infidels. He conquered the fort Qamus during battle of Khyber in 7 A.H., where other Muslim warriors and experts of war failed. In other battles also he proved his bravery by exemplary achievements.

Caliphate

After the martyrdom of Hadrat 'Usman (R.A.A.) on 18th Zil-Hijja, 35 A.H., Hadrat Zubair and Hadrat Talha (R.A.A.) came to Hadrat 'Ali (R.A.A.) along with a group of Muhajireen and Ansar and desired for taking Oath of Allegiance in his favour, In view of the disturbed condition, he hesitated to accept the office of Caliph and advised them to select any one else. They insisted on their request as in their opinion, he was the most rightful person for the august position. On their persistent pressure, he came to the mosque and announced general invitation for taking Oath of Allegiance to him. First of all, Hadrat Talha and Hadrat Zubair took the Oath of Allegiance on the condition that his caliphate would be amdinistered on the injunctions of Quran and Sunnah and he would establish the punishments fixed by the Shariah. It implied that he would punish the assassinators of Hadrat 'Usman (R.A.A.). Thereafter, many people offered Oath of Allegiance to him.

The other day, both Hadrat Talha and Hadrat Zubair

(R.A.A.) demanded for punishment of the assassinators of Hadrat 'Usman (R.A.A.). Hadrat 'Ali said that neither the assassinators had so far been traced out nor he had gained strength by that time, let the administration be settled, then the matter would be taken up. The proposition of Hadrat 'Ali (R.A.A.) created a suspicion among people about his future line of action. Unfortunately, during this period he appointed Maalik bin Ashtar and Muhammad bin Abi Bakr, as his advisers and key men who were known ring leaders of the assassinators of Hadrat Usman (R.A.A.). This confirmed the people's doubts. Soon, Hadrat Zubair and Hadrat Talha (R.A.A.) asked his permission to proceed to Makkah, which was granted.

In Makkah, they consulted the people, especially Mother of the Faithful Hadrat Ayesha (R.A.A.), who was already enraged on the incident. Consequently a huge army of about 3000, under the leadership of Hadrat Ayesha (R.A.A.), left for Basrah and after a fight with the governor of Basrah, appointed by Hadrat 'Ali (R.A.A.), defeated him. Thus on 14 Rabi-ul-Aakhir, 36 A.H. Basrah fell to them.

Battle of Jamal -36 A.H.

Hadrat 'Ali (R.A.A.) decided to invade Basrah and fight with Hadrat Ayesha (R.A.A.), and others. the noble companions of the Prophet (S.A.W.) advised Hadrat 'Ali (R.A.A.) to abandon his programme but he rejected. The people of Kufa allied with Hadrat 'Ali's army. He arrived at Basrah with his army and after prolonged negotiations between the two forces, the fight started.

During the fight, Hadrat 'Ali got a chance to reach close to Hadrat Zubair and reminded him of the advice of Holy Prophet (S.A.W.). On hearing this, Hadrat Zubair (R.A.A.) repented, withdrew from fight, and left for Madinah. Hadrat Talha (R.A.A.) observed this and followed suit but the patrons of fight killed him by shooting a poisoned arrow. The fight was furious and about 10,000 Muims fell martyred. Hadrat 'Ali

(R.A.A.) gained victory. In this fight, Hadrat Ayesha (R.A.A.) was riding on camel, called "Jamal" in Arabic; therefore this battle was known as 'Battle of Jamal'.

Battle of Siffin - 37 A.H.

After Battle of Jamal, Hadrat 'Ali (R.A.A.) turned towards the Syrians and made preparations to fight Hadrat Mu'awiya (R.A.A.). He first tried to settle the issue by negotiations but all in vain. Consequently, he started for combat and first encamped at Nukhaila, where Hadrat Abdullah bin Abbas (R.A.A.) arrived with his army. Hadrat 'Ali (R.A.A.) then proceeded towards Syria and after corssing the Euphrates encamped at Siffin. Hadrat Mu'awiya (R.A.A.) also arrived there with Hadrat 'Amr bin al-Aas (R.A.A.) and other Syrian expert fighters. Hadrat Mu'awiya (R.A.A.) demanded from Hadrat 'Ali (R.A.A.) to hand over to him the assassinators of Hadrat 'Usman (R.A.A.) whereupon the latter asked him first to offer his allegiance and then raise the issue of retaliation. However, on failure to reach any sattlement, the fight started. After a temporary peace on the appearance of the moon of Muharram, 37 A.H.., an attempt was made again to solve the issue but in vain. Hadrat 'Ali (R.A.A.) declared in the month of Safar that since enough time had been given to Syrians for consideration, and now formal war would begin tomorrow to settle the issue. War started on 8th Safar and continued on 9th. There was a furious fighting. On that day, when the Syrians were about to be uprooted, Hadrat Mu'awiya and Hadrat 'Amr bin al'-Aas (R.A.A.) proved their foresight, i.e. Syrian raised high the Quran on spears and requested to base decision on it. Seeing this, the Kufis held their hands back from fight. This is known as battle of Siffin, in which 70,000 Muslims were martyred from both sides.

Afterwards, in negotiation to settle the issue in the light of Quran and Traditions, controversies arose and the note of agreement prepared on 13 Safar was opposed by about 4000 people of Ghazah tribe and others. Hadrat 'Ali (R.A.A.) did not support the idea of backing out from the agreement and departed to Kufa from Siffin. However, on the persistence of people, Hadrat Abu Musa Ash'ari (R.A.A.) from the side of Hadrat 'Ali (R.A.A.) and Hadrat Amar bin al-'Aas from the side of Hadrat Mu'awiya (R.A.A.) were appointed as members for arbitration committee and it was decided that the decision on the issue would be delivered after 6 months at Doo-ma-tul-jandal. When Hadrat 'Ali (R.A.A.) arrived at Kufa, 12000 soldiers, who were against the decision, separated from him and left Kufa, established military centre at field of Harurah and made Ash'as bin Rabi'i their leader. This group was against Hadrat 'Ali (R.A.A.) as well as Hadrat Mu'awiya (R.A.A.) both. From the field of Harurah, they started their movement and were called Khawarij (Separatists).

On the other side, the arbitration committee's decision went in favour of Hadrat Mu'awiya and against Hadrat 'Ali (R.A.A.) and was rejected by the latter. This further made the situation grim and the division among Hadrat 'Ali's own companions strengthened Khawarij. They asked Hadrat 'Ali (R.A.A.) to accept mistake in honouring the agreement and offer his repentance, otherwise they would fight with him. They appointed Abdullah bin Wahab al-Raasi as their leader and moved towards Basrah, Anbar and Madain, propagating against Hadrat 'Ali and killing his supporters. When Hadrat 'Ali got the news, he, instead of going to Syria, turned towards them and reached Nah'ravan with his army. First he tried to correct them by prayer and preach, but when they did not agree, he started war against them (in 38 A.H.). The Khawarij were defeated. This fighting is knowing as battle on Nah'ravan.

Martyrdom

After the Battle of Nah'ravan, among the Khawarij who escaped death, Adbul Rahman bin Muljim, Bark bin Abd and Amr bin Bakr Al-Taimi, gathered in Hijaz and conspired to relieve the Muslims from the oppression of the three pervasive leaders (Ali, Mu'awiya and Amr bin al-Aas) by killing them. Ibn Muljim, Bark and Amr each planned to kill 'Ali, Mu'awiya and 'Amr bin al-'Aas (R.A.A.) respectively, and also pledged to return after completing their task and fixed 17th Ramazan 40 A.H. at morning prayers, to accomplish their plan. Ibn Muljim fatally wounded Hadrat 'Ali (R.A.A.), when he entered the mosque for "Fajr" (Morning) prayers. He was arrested but Hadrat Ali advised, "if I die then Ibn Muljim shall be killed in retaliation but his dead body may not be trampled upon by horses because Holy Prophet (S.A.W.) has forbidden it. If I remain alive, I will deal with him as I may like". Then he gave some advices to his sons and breathed his last (Inna lil-la-he-wa-inna ilai-he raje'oon). He was buried in Kufa at Dar-ul-Aman.

Age and Period of Caliphate of Hadrat 'Ali (R.A.A.)

Hadrat 'Ali (R.A.A.) attained the age of 63 (also reported 68) years and span of his caliphate was about 4-3/4 years, which mostly passed in dealing with the internal disturbances and domestic feuds.

Heritage of Hadrat 'Ali (R.A.A.)

When he passed away, he left only seven or eight hundred Dirhams (equal to about Rs.200/-).

Wives and Children of Hadrat 'Ali (R.A.A.)

Hadrat Fatimah (R.A.A.) was Hadrat 'Ali's first wife and during her life, he did not marry any other woman. After her death, he married nine women on different occasions.

He had 31 children - 14 sons and 17 daughters. From Hadrat Fatimah he had 3 sons—Hadrat Hasan, Hadrat Husain and Mohsin (who died in childhood) and two daughters-Zainab al Kubra and Umm Kulsoom Kubra. The remaining children were born from other wives and slave-girls. However, the genealogy of Hadrat 'Ali continued from Hadrat Hasan, Hadrat Husain, Hadrat Muhammad Hanfiah, Hadrat Umar, and Hadrat

Abbas (R.A.A.)

Features

He was of short stature with brownish complexion, large eyes and handsome blooming face. He had plenty of hair on his chest. His body was strong, well-shaped and smart. The muscles of his arms and legs were fleshy and he kept his head always shaved.

His Manners and Habits

He possessed pleasing habits, cheerful disposition, wily nature and polite temperament. He always spoke to people with smiling conutenance and liveliness. During conversation, he used humorous clauses. He was so perfect in his habits that when the Prophet (S.A.W.) cut joke with him he replied to him in the same style. He was always seen smiling. He was so humble that he made all household purchases by himself, visiting the markets, helped the labourers in lifting their loads and guided the persons led astray.

He was so gentle and forgiving that he pardoned even serious mistakes of people and did not punish them. He was so particular about the safety of wealth of people that he dismissed his cousin Hadrat Abbas (R.A.A.) from governorship on a little doubt of misappropriation. Always, he audited the account of the public treasury to a penny and never spent even a small amount on his person. He was so simple that he earned his livelihood by toil and labour. He grazed camels, stitched his shoes and excavated the ground with a spade by himself.

His Attainments in Knowledge

No historical evidence of his education is available but his accomplishments in the field of all arts, indicate perfect management of his education. The various science and arts in which he attained distinctive position are as under :

1) Science of Reciting Quran
2) Science of Commentary of Quran
3) Knowledge of Islamic law of Inheritance
4) Science of Mysticism
5) Science of Logic
6) Science of Grammar
7) Art of Calligraphy
8) Art of Oratory
9) Art of Poetry

Dress of Hadrat 'Ali (R.A.A.)

He lived a very simple life although he was a sovereign ruler of the world of Islam and controller of public treasury. He usually wore a 'Kurta' (long shirt) made of coarse cotton cloth and short Tahband (Loin cloth—sheet of cloth worn round the waist to cover lower portion of body). These dresses contained patches of repairs. People tried their best to persuade him to obtain some money from the public treasury to wear nice clothes but he rejected the proposal. Turban was his favourite head dress.